Mike Kleist

The Secret to Male Multiple Orgasms and other sex skills

www.mancan.net

Mike Kleist, a banker, master of communication science and advertising psychology, dedicated himself intensively, even during his student years, to sexual research, in theory and practice. During his research, he hit upon the centuries-old secret knowledge of Asian cultures, and developed, in conjunction with modern scientific knowledge, a training program that enables every man to learn how to have multiple orgasms. This well-rounded free spirit is also a professional skydiver. As a camera-flyer and athlete he competed in several national and international Championships in various disciplines (Freefly, Freestyle, Skysurfing, Canopy Piloting). As a professional trainer and coach he helps clients to improve and bring more joy to their lives. Further he holds a university teaching postition at the University of Munich and teaches public speaking and presentation techniques.

Cover Design: Mike Kleist

Graphics: Mike Kleist, Amir Moye

Translation: Mark Pettus

Final editing: Mike Kleist

Original edition

Published by love-skills.com

Printer:
Lulu Enterprises Inc.
860 Aviation Parkway
Suite 300
Morrisville, NC 27560
United States of America

ISBN: 978-3-00-026971-4

This book can be found in any bookstore or on the Internet on

www.mancan.net

Contents

A Joke, For Starters

Adam is sitting around in Paradise and hears God sigh: “That’s tough, that’s tough…”
Adam: “What’s the deal?”
The Lord God: “Well, I still have two skills to divide between you and Eve.”
Adam: “And what are they?”
The Lord God: “The first is the ability to piss while standing.”
Adam: “Oh, please let it be me! I’ve just got to be able to do that… that sounds fantastic… please, please, please let me be able to piss while standing!”
The Lord God: “Let it be thus!”

And with that, Adam left his mark on every single tree and bush in Paradise, and gloated over his new ability…

When he finally returned to the Lord God, he wondered: “And what was the other one?

The Lord God: “Multiple orgasms!

Illustration 1: Adam & Eve perform their given skills

1. Introduction

Yeah, Adam got a bit ahead of himself there. But the good news is that although "Eves" may enjoy mastery of the multiple orgasm from birth, any "Adam" can also learn this art, with a little practice and the right technique.

I could hardly believe it when I first heard of the male multiple orgasm. A friend next to me at a row of urinals asked me, as we were pissing (while standing): "Can you piss in squirts?" Taken aback, I answered: "Heck yeah… why do you ask?" He smirked and said: "Then I've got a little something for you that will revolutionize your sex life! With a little practice, you can have multiple orgasms. Never again will you have to hold yourself back in order to wait on your special lady. You can maintain your erection after orgasm, and come yet again. Total control!" I asked, "Can you do that?" He grinned: "Heck yeah! Let me give you a book that I accidentally got my hands on a while back."

At first I couldn't believe it. Sure, I had heard before that there were supposedly men who had superhuman "erectile powers," and I'd also heard rumors of men who could come several times in a row. But from my point of view, these were "Supermen" who had been blessed at birth with a wonderful gift. I was of the opinion that multiple orgasms were a lot like penis length: either one was blessed, or one wasn't.

In any case, I knew from personal experience that I myself lost my erection after one orgasm, and was only able to recuperate the necessary "standing ability" a considerable time later. And now I was hearing that supposedly anyone can learn not only to maintain an erection, but also to experience several orgasms. I was very skeptical, but also curious. Without a doubt, I wanted to delve more deeply into this secret.

The book my friend gave me opened my eyes! It was a whole new world for me, and I was captivated by the new possibilities that this knowledge revealed. Subsequently, I've been much occupied with this topic. I researched to learn as much as possible about male multiple orgasm. And I found numerous scientific treatments and research reports that supported this thesis. Unfortunately, they were often very dense, and were made difficult to read by their scientific style.

I became like a sponge, sucking up all of this knowledge hOn the side, I conducted various exercises, some of which worked better than others. During this time, the sponge has become so full that I can now express its content, and summarize, in this book, the best of literature, science, and my own experience.

It was important to me that the book be easy to read, and that it be of great practical usefulness for the reader. I want to convey concentrated knowledge in a way that would be as easy to understand as possible. And so, in the present book, medical terminology, foreign words and scientifically inflated sentences are avoided. But this says nothing about the quality of the knowledge being conveyed. The content is "highly potent," and whoever wants to can find in the list of sources books and works on this topic that treat portions of this book in a more scientific, and more complicated, manner. The main thing for me is that the reader learns what's important, and, hopefully, has fun doing it.

Since we're dealing with a topic that's "below the belt," and since we'll be spending a fair amount of time together, I suggest that we speak to each other as friends. So, follow me now, and let me initiate you into the "secret knowledge" of the male multiple orgasm!

Advice for female readers:

I'm glad that you're interested in this book. After all, you're the one who will end up benefiting from your partner's newfound abilities. This book should provide you and your partner with longer-lasting and more stimulating sex, thereby helping to increase your level of intimacy. Support your partner in his efforts. Most importantly, you can actively help your partner during the partner exercises. Have no fear – the exercises aren't some sort of mechanical lessons to go through. They're exercises that should be a lot of fun for you, and bring you a sense of closeness – and you'll certainly get a great return on your investment.

A tip for you: Do all the exercises for yourself. It'll be well worth it. You'll get to know yourself and your body better. You'll come to better understand your own stimulation, and that of your partner, and you'll learn how to increase it with the help of these exercises. You too can set out on this adventure!

Advice for homosexual readers:

Although this book is written from a heterosexual point of view, the knowledge and ability, as well as all the exercises, can, of course, be completely carried over to a homosexual relationship. And in this case, the benefit is doubled, since both partners will benefit from it equally!

How to Use this Book

The book will convey knowledge in an entertaining fashion. Therefore, you will encounter a lot of metaphors in this book that will convey the material as graphically as possible, and hopefully elicit a laugh or two.

I recommend that you keep a pen or marker handy, to take notes or to mark certain sections. The text is divided into many paragraphs. This should make it easy to read, and make it simpler for you to highlight particular sections. So, the more marks and notes you make in the book, the more valuable it will become for you.

You can also prepare mind-maps for particular chapters. This visual learning method is much more efficient for most people than written text. When doing so, write down important key words on a sheet of paper and try to link them by drawing lines, according to their interrelations. In this way, you'll get a good overview of the ways in which they are connected – a bird's-eye-view, so to speak. The more you work with this technique, the easier it will become for you. (I myself successfully use mind-maps for important books, information, and solutions to problems.)

You'll find several exercises in this book. The important thing here is to go through them in order, and not to skip any exercise. There are no shortcuts here, since the exercises have been carefully chosen, and build upon each other. Before you start on an exercise, you should read through it carefully once more – best of all, together with your partner. When doing partner exercises the two of you can clarify all open questions beforehand. At the end of each description, the most important points are summarized once again.

Sex can be very demanding. Older people should adapt the exercises to their endurance and fitness level. In the case of heart problems, the training should be discussed beforehand with a doctor.

One more tip regarding the use of this book: it makes a great gift. As a wedding present, for example, it will not only provide a good laugh right off the bat, but will also have an enduring effect on the couple's entire future. Just think about it!

There's a lot of new material waiting to be discovered in this book that may contradict your previous point of view. Therefore, I'd like to close the instructions for using this book with the request that you use your mind like a parachute. Because this, too, works best when it's open.

Internet Forum

On my web site, www.mancan.net I offer a forum where you can share your experiences, tips and tricks, exercise variations, and criticism with other readers. Access to the forum is restricted and the password is: MOforum (case sensitive)

2. The Sexual Revolution: Man and Woman

In the past thirty years, women have experienced a sexual revolution. Whereas their sexual pleasure was almost completely taboo before the 1960s, the literature of the past decades has occupied itself almost exclusively with the newly won sexual self-consciousness of women. Since that time, the female orgasm has been front and center for many sexual advisers.

As welcome as this development may be, it places men, consciously or unconsciously, under pressure. Men feel a certain responsibility for providing women with maximum satisfaction. The number of orgasms that a man can provide for a woman thus becomes a performance indicator of the man's sexual abilities. Premature ejaculation leads to frustration for many men and women.

This development has had positive effects in terms of the expansion of foreplay. Men "discover" alternative techniques, of an oral or nimble-fingered nature. Nevertheless, it's hard for many of them to experience a simultaneous orgasm, since the "timing" can often present difficulties.

Who hasn't experienced it: you're in the middle of love-making, and you're doing your best. You struggle not to get too close to your own orgasm, since you'd like to give her one was well. She slowly approaches her climax and cries out, "yes, harder!" or "don't stop!" or "more, more, just like that!" You know that if you maintain the desired tempo, or even accelerate it, premature ejaculation is unavoidable.

On the other hand, you don't want to slow down the tempo, and thereby interrupt her rhythm. For her, that's like slamming on the brakes just before the finish line – and that's equally unsatisfying.

Many advisers recommend that men think of something else (as un-erotic as possible), in order to restrain their own arousal and avoid a premature orgasm. But hey, let's be honest: who, when engaged in the "most beautiful leisure activity in the world," wants to think in a calculated fashion about something un-erotic?

Besides, it seems a lot like a struggle with one's own body. Meanwhile, satisfaction– at least for the man – falls by the wayside.

What should you do? The solution to the problem is conceivably simple: "come" and keep on going! Now, you might be thinking: "Say what? By then my erection's long gone! You can't play pick-up-sticks with wet spaghetti noodles!"

The male multiple orgasm offers a way out of this situation. You'll learn how to maintain your erection after orgasm, and go on to experience a new climax. This book should bring pleasure equally to both men and women. In buying this book, you're showing your readiness to learn a new technique that, first and foremost, will benefit your partner. Perhaps, for that very same reason, you may have received it as a gift.

Once you've learned it, the ability to have multiple orgasms will relieve you of the burden of that "sword of Damocles" – the premature ejaculation. You'll learn to have total control over your level of arousal and your erection. Your partner will profit from it – and besides that, it will increase the sense of intimacy through the length of time and the enjoyment that the two of you will now be able to enjoy, in an entirely new way.

Meanwhile, you're surely asking yourself, impatiently, "How?" We're just getting to that! But first we need to dispense with a couple of "old yarns," and get rid of certain misunderstandings. More on that in the following chapter.

3. Sexual Myths

As I already mentioned in the introduction, I too was convinced that I was incapable of learning how to achieve multiple orgasms. But aside from this misunderstanding, I encountered, in my research, other sexual myths that I had previously taken at face value. A relevant saying, applicable not only to this topic, is: The head is round so the thoughts can change direction.

So, prepare yourself to learn something new in this chapter – something that, perhaps, will contradict your old convictions. Because the following knowledge is the foundation for the ability to have multiple orgasms, and to learn how to have them.

One further bit of wisdom that can be applied to this topic, as well as to many others, was expressed by Albert Einstein: "The problems we're facing today cannot be solved with the same level of thinking that we had, when we created them."

The problem, in our case, is limiting oneself to a single orgasm. So, we'll do just as Albert suggests: we'll discard our previous point of view, and be on the lookout for a better one. You won't believe it, but I happen to have a couple of them up my sleeve.

Myth No. 1: Orgasm = Ejaculation

The most important misunderstanding, in light of our topic, is the belief, still extremely widespread, that orgasm and ejaculation are one and the same. **This is absolutely false!** True, ejaculation usually does directly follow orgasm (by 0.5-2 seconds), but still, these are two completely independent experiences.

This distinction is so important because it makes multiple orgasms possible in the first place. But how did we arrive at this myth, which even sexual researchers long held to be true?

To answer this question, it is necessary to take a look at sexual development during youth.

Development During Puberty

Children treat their sexuality relatively spontaneously, until they learn from their parents and their society that "you can't touch yourself there," or "you can't speak openly about something like that." Some detect that the parents themselves are uncomfortable speaking about self-satisfaction, while others never even have the pleasure of talking to their parents about it even to a limited extent. The result is a feeling of insecurity, even fear. Especially when it comes to one's first ejaculations.

Of course, most children have already experienced orgasms by exploring their own bodies. It is a yet-unknown feeling of pleasure that nothing can compare with. And it works so simply. And even after the first peak of excitement, it is possible to repeat the feeling of pleasure through further arousal.

The first ejaculation, on the other hand, is a shock for many children. Anyone who hasn't already heard something about this natural bodily function reacts with a shameful bewilderment that borders on panicked fear. True, the feeling of joy upon reaching a climax remains the same, but the release of semen leads to many different things: on the one hand, the embarrassment that the stains can bring, and on the other, the difficulty of repeating the feeling of pleasure. Sperm that's spend brings the end.

Many men – who today are multi-orgasmic – tried even as youths to avoid ejaculation. With a bit of effort, they could enjoy the same climax as before, without having the ejaculation bring a premature end to their pleasure. These men learned the ability to have multiple orgasms on their own; for them, this is something that is completely natural.

But that's the exception. Most children resign themselves to their "fate" and take it as a given that a single climax is sufficient.

Orgasm and Ejaculation

Orgasm itself is defined as a climax of emotional and physical reactions. The pulse rises briefly, and falls again following the orgasm. The pelvic muscle contracts. At the same time, the spectrum of feelings ranges from a warm prickling to a sense of becoming one with the universe.

Ejaculation, on the other hand, may be divided into three separate phases. In the first phase, the testicles rise and are brought into the position required for ejaculation. The prostate, vas deferens, and sphincter contract. This phase of ejaculation is also called the contraction phase. Through these and other contractions of the pelvic muscle, the sperm is, in the so-called expulsion phase, pressed through the vas deferens and shot out of the penis.

After the actual ejaculation, the so-called refraction phase sets in: an oversensitivity of the glans, a drop of blood engorgement, and, along with it, a loss of erection, a sinking of the testicles, as well as a feeling of relaxation that borders on lethargy.

This rather superficial account of what happens during orgasm and ejaculation should make clear that these are two independent events that may follow one another, but do not have to. I promised you from the start that I wouldn't bore you with detailed medical descriptions. And what's really important when it comes to learning how to achieve multiple orgasms isn't any knowledge of anatomical details, but only the fact that orgasm and ejaculation aren't the same thing. Ejaculation is a reflex that is triggered by orgasm. Controlling this reflex is the path to multiple orgasms.

You will learn techniques that will allow you to delay ejaculation and nevertheless experience an orgasm. The refraction phase connected with ejaculation is thereby avoided, and the erection continues to stand tall.

The sexual researchers Hartman and Fithian are of the following opinion concerning this misunderstanding: "We are convinced that the only thing preventing a man from experiencing multiple orgasms stems from a conviction resulting from his upbringing, and from his acceptance of the fixed idea that orgasm and ejaculation must always coincide for a man."

Myth No. 2: Only Women Can Have Multiple Orgasms

The second myth we must free ourselves from is the belief that only women can have multiple orgasms. You'll soon learn that a woman's orgasm is, generally speaking, very similar to a man's. But first, a brief excursion into history.

Society's Treatment of the Orgasm

About 100 years ago, women who had an orgasm were morally despised. Only prostitutes and other sexually questionable women were thought to have fun during sex. "Respectable" women regarded sex as a conjugal duty. If they enjoyed it, it wasn't considered appropriate to show it.

As has already been mentioned in the "sexual revolution" chapter, all this has, fortunately, changed. Over the years, women have achieved more sexual self-determination. Women, as well as the literature, discovered the orgasm, which more and more women were able to enjoy. But women enjoying multiple orgasms were still the exception at the beginning of this development. Men, concerned mostly with their own satisfaction, rarely held out long enough to allow this phenomenon to manifest itself.

Only around 50 years ago did the female orgasm come to be considered normal. As a result, one learned that women who were further stimulated after the first orgasm could have further climaxes. This was confirmed by research on the subject, which began around 30 years ago. Hardly any attention was paid to the male orgasm.

But here, too, there seemed to be a mental barrier similar to the one seen in the development of female sexuality. Determined by Christian belief, which held that the only purpose of sex was procreation, it was accepted that men could only have one orgasm, which accompanied ejaculation. Research, too, took this as a given, and no pains were taken to dispute it.

Orgasm Research

The sexual researchers Hartman and Fithian were the first to purposefully take up the male orgasm, beginning in the late 70s. Scientifically speaking, they were exploring new territory, and were mocked at first by many colleagues, who attributed no meaning to their thesis regarding male multiple orgasm. But in the end, their success justified them. Through their research, they showed not only that the male multiple orgasm is possible, but also that it is learnable.

A similar finding was made independently by the scientists Robbins and Jensen, in their 1978 article entitled "Multiple Orgasms in Males." But Hartman and Fithian were the first to carry out a large-scale study on the topic. They examined 740 individuals, of whom 282 were men. Of these, 33 were multi-orgasmic. The reactions of the examined individuals were recorded during masturbation as well as during sexual intercourse.

In the process, it was shown that the curves which resulted from measuring the pulse were almost the same in men and women. During orgasm, the pulse rises briefly, only to sink again quickly thereafter. The length of time occupied by an orgasm is basically between 6 and 30 seconds. The time taken to reach an orgasm is very different for all people, and varies from 2 minutes to as long as an hour.

There are two kinds of multiple orgasms.

• **Discrete multiple orgasms** –here, the pulse sinks back to its original level

• **Continuous multiple orgasms** – here, the pulse does not sink back to its baseline, but remains high.

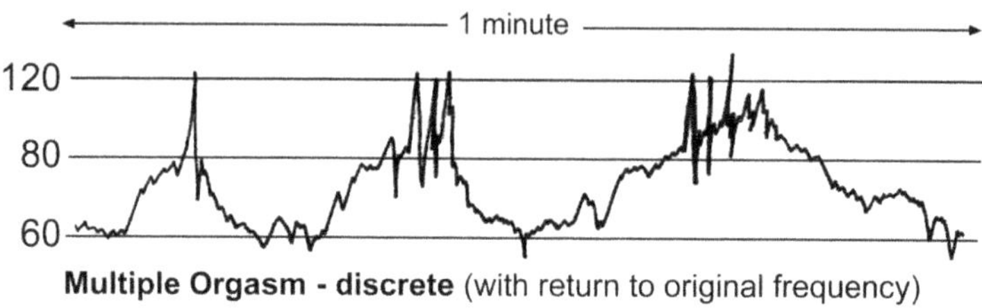

Multiple Orgasm - discrete (with return to original frequency)

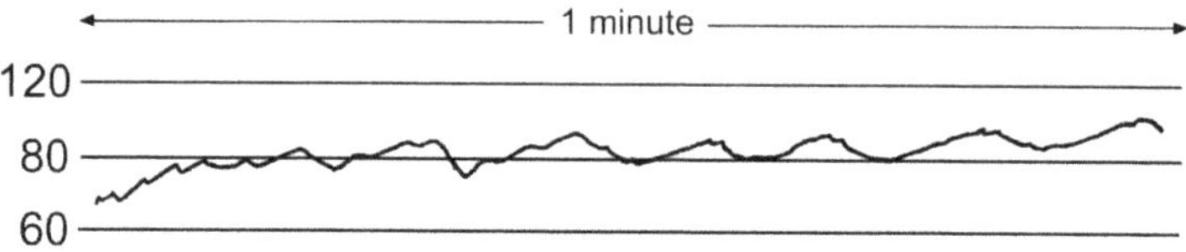

Multiple Orgasm - continuous (without return to original frequency)

Illustration 2: discrete and continuous multiple orgasms (Source: Hartman and Fithian)

Both kinds of orgasm were registered in women as well as in multi-orgasmic men. Moreover, the pulse-curves of men and women were very similar.

It follows from this that men too can have multiple orgasms, if they are in a position to avoid ejaculation and the refraction phase that goes along with it. You'll learn the ways in which you can avoid ejaculation in chapter 5.

Myth No. 3: "Dry" Orgasms Are Less Satisfying

This is the place to do away with yet another prejudice that one often hears when men are confronted with the fact that orgasm and ejaculation are two separate things: orgasms without ejaculation are less satisfying.

This is just ignorance speaking, and perhaps a little envy as well. In fact, the exact opposite is true! Because of the feeling of tiredness brought about by the refraction phase following ejaculation, the "dry" orgasm is actually more satisfying. Many men even do without ejaculation completely, because they wish to avoid the loss of energy connected with it. Anyone who regards sex purely as a means of blowing off some steam may see ejaculation as the greater satisfaction. But anyone who has sex because of the fun it provides finds ejaculation to be the less satisfying event, especially when it brings an unplanned end to lovemaking.

Anyone who has learned the ability to have multiple orgasms will never want to do without it. During the "training phase," restraining ejaculation may still seem to be something you're not used to, or find demanding. But anyone who has really mastered the technique knows how satisfying "dry orgasms" can be as well. Once you've learned it, the effort required is so slight, and the control over your own body so great, that you can no longer do without it. Further along, I'll show you techniques that allow you to spread your orgasms throughout your entire body. Then, the pelvic orgasm will become an orgasm of the body itself. But more on this later.

Being able to better satisfy one's partner is also not the only reason to prolong love-making. Many multi-orgasmic men, myself included, use this technique during masturbation as well, in order to prolong their own enjoyment. This should be argument enough for anyone, since it contributes, above all, to one's own satisfaction.

Whether with or without ejaculation, orgasms are satisfying, each in its own way. But it's a nice feeling to have a choice!

Why Almost No One Knows the "Secret"

One question you've probably already asked yourself is: How is it that this ability is "secret knowledge?" Well, it's hardly secret, of course. It's merely a bit of knowledge that doesn't spread all by itself. Sexual development plays out very differently over the centuries, according to the cultural sphere. The next chapter offers a brief overview.

Historical Development

The first known indications come from China, where this knowledge was kept secret by noblemen and wealthy merchants. For this reason, one point in the genital region is tellingly referred to by Chinese teaching as the "point of a million gold coins" (more on this later). This knowledge was very precious at the time, and was therefore guarded. Back then, it was indeed a piece of "secret knowledge". Much like Kung Fu, students were trained by a master in order to be initiated into its secrets.

The first "public writing" to deal with this topic was the "Tao of Love." According to it as well, this knowledge was reserved for the upper classes, since education and the ability to read were a privilege. The emphasis was on prolonging the sexual encounter between a man and a woman. This can occur with or without sexual intercourse, and brings both to a state of spiritual ecstasy.

The "Tantra" is viewed as the Indian equivalent of the "Tao of Love." The Tantra is, in its sexual descriptions, heavily dependent on the religious practices of the time. The man's semen was considered holy, and it was viewed as harmful to one's health to squander it. Practices were described that a man could use to bring his ejaculations under control. Prolonging sex was achieved, much as was the case in the "Tao of Love," by avoiding ejaculation. However, this does not have as a consequence a limitation of the number of orgasms.

A further technique practiced in numerous cultures is the "retrograde ejaculation." This means that the ejaculation is purposefully redirected back into the bladder. This can happen by straining the sphincter, or by pressing with the fingers. An external ejaculation does not take place. The ejaculate is then passed out the next time one urinates, without any side effects for one's health. For a wide circle of cultures, this was an effective method of birth control. But since an ejaculation takes place with this technique nevertheless, the erection typically disappears. It is therefore less suited for multiple orgasms. We'll have more to say about this phenomenon in the exercise section, since it can happen, during multiple orgasm training, that the orgasm is indeed "dry," but the erection gives way nonetheless. More on that later.

So, the man's semen was considered holy in many cultures.

Despite that fact, sexual enjoyment was treated more permissively than was the case in the Christian world. Prolonging the sex act was even a component of religious sexuality. Techniques were therefore developed that made it possible for men to enjoy sexual pleasures without spilling their precious semen.

Unlike in the West, well-to-do men in Eastern cultures were able to have several wives. This was even considered a status symbol, both financially and sexually. Anyone who could provide for and satisfy several wives was held in very high esteem. Thus, an incentive simultaneously arose to increase one's sexual ability, either by delaying orgasm or by having multiple orgasms.

The Influence of Christianity

"Be fruitful and multiply"... but don't have any fun doing it. Christianity preached the procreative aspect of sexuality exclusively. Christendom held sexual lust, or ecstasy, to be a sin: the masses were controlled through the demonization of physical pleasures. The church aroused feelings of guilt whose grip is felt even today. For many, masturbation itself, or even touching the genitals with one's hand, is sinful.

One must free oneself from these value judgments, since they lack all foundation, apart from hardheadedness. While the procreation incentive was still understandable in time periods with high death rates among infants, our concern with regard to population has long since become the exact opposite. Birth control is now necessary to get a handle on overpopulation. On this score, the church even hears criticism from among its own ranks, when, for example, it forbids contraceptives in Third World countries.

But the church has always manufactured a chasm between rich and poor. In the Middle Ages, the rich were taught to read, while the poor were purposefully left ignorant. Even back then, sexual pleasure served as a distraction for the rich, and was tolerated by the church, while the pleasures of the body were portrayed to the poor as unclean and sinful.

Sex is an important part of love, and of life. Anyone who wants to advance and reach a higher level of physical pleasure must free himself from any and all feelings of guilt. Everything is allowed, as long as it is pleasing for both partners, and arises not out of force, but out of love and desire. Then sex is the most pleasurable way to exchange positive energy.

Why Almost No One Arrives at Multiple Orgasms On Their Own

In our culture, the sexual development of a young man is still often taboo. During the first sexual experiences with one's own body, most boys, conditioned by a bad conscience, masturbate "on the sly." The fear of being caught is too great.

Since the technique they learn leads to "success" (orgasm), there is little reason to experiment further or to change one's technique in retrospect. Especially since there are no indications that, if used differently, it can "work" even better. Those who learn to become multi-orgasmic during puberty consider it just as natural as those men who have made do with a single orgasm. An exchange between these two groups seldom occurs.

Since only a very few know that men can have multiple orgasms, and that this ability can be learned, no one makes a conscious effort to obtain the relevant information. More than likely, you too have hit on this book by accident. Let me tell you: this was probably the best "spontaneous purchase" of your life.

Sex Sells

Another possible reason for the slow discovery of this secret in this day and age is, perhaps, the commercialization of sex. Through the media, such as the Internet and television, we are flooded with sexual stimulation. Time is money. The quick fulfillment of our desires is promised everywhere.

But is this really our goal? In the porn industry, the so-called "cum-shot" (the footage showing the ejaculation) is the measure of all things – the climax – the proof of orgasm.

It's hard to go against the grain and declare that orgasm and ejaculation have little to do with each other, that it isn't, in fact, ejaculation that is a sign of masculine energy, but rather the delaying of the expulsion of semen - for more orgasms, and, thereby, manifold satisfaction. For the man, and for the woman as well. I'm no moralizer, and have no intention to rob anyone of their enjoyment of pornography. I'd only like to open your eyes, so that you'll recognize how you're being manipulated. Keep in mind that porn films are all artificially orchestrated to the rythm of a man's hand and cannot do justice to the complexity of a genuine, ecstatic sexuality.

Take the time for sex. Whether it's pleasuring yourself, or having sex with a partner – the satisfaction you experience as a result will, in any case, increase.

The simple formula here is:

Several orgasms are better than one!

Sex is fun!

More time = more fun!

4. Penis & Co. – The Tools For Success

You've already learned the real secret. It consists of the fact that orgasm and ejaculation aren't one and the same. That's great, you say, but where does that get me? Well, this knowledge is the basis for all further techniques. Namely, these aim to establish this separation – or, more precisely, to avoid ejaculation and have an orgasm nonetheless. An orgasm? No, several! The advantage to avoiding ejaculation is that the erection is maintained. And that opens the door to further orgasms. As many as your heart desires!

This chapter is a very special anatomical lesson. The goal is to extract the maximum pleasure from your "tools." In order to do that, you first need to get to know them better, and you'll probably also discover a couple of new ones that, until now, you've been neglecting. Not all of them are necessary in order to learn the art of multiple orgasm, but all of them can, in addition, provide you with worlds of fun. So it's well worth it to take a theoretical side-trip.

In the next chapter, the M.O. technique is described – that is, the task of the "tools." Then, at last, we'll be done with the theory, and ready to move on to the practice: step by step, to the multiple orgasm.

But first, we must turn to an old acquaintance:

The Penis. That Unknown Creature

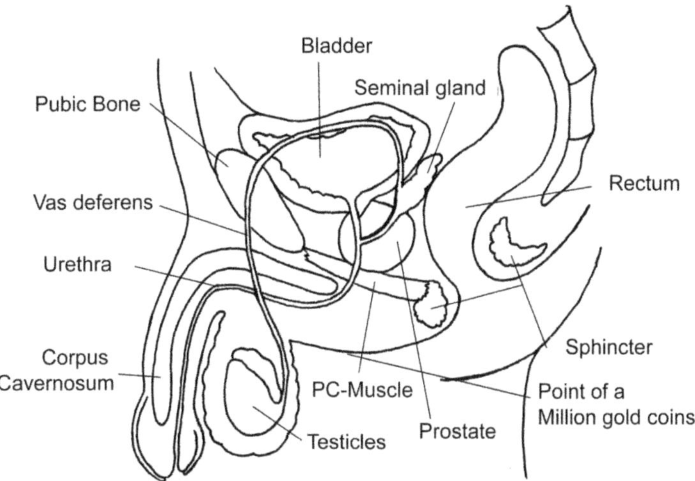

Illustration 3: The Penis

Your penis is one of your most long-standing acquaintances. The two of you are very close; you lend it a helping hand on a daily basis. Nevertheless, many men have a love-hate relationship with their penis. Too big, too small, too thick, too thin or even crooked – rare indeed is the man who is fully satisfied with its appearance. And yet, many men identify with their penis. They give it a name, or even talk to it. And why do men give their penis a name? Because it's nice to know the name of the one who's calling the shots. But all jokes aside.

This estranged relationship leads men to treat their penis as a foreign entity. They even ascribe to it a will of its own – a will that most often rears its head (or rather, doesn't) when the man himself wants things done completely differently. This can lead to moments fraught with embarrassment. Like an erection in the sauna, for example, or the lack thereof precisely when one needs it the most – during lovemaking. The fear of their own reactions that men develop as a result leads, in the end, to self-fulfilling prophecies, and to a state of affairs in which the penis wags the man.

In fact, it should be the other way around. You yourself want to have control over your penis. But in order for that to happen, you must first come to accept it for what it is. Learn to view it as a part of your body, not as some independent being.

Take it for what it is, and be proud of it. It's one-of-a-kind! That being done, you can also learn to control it, instead of being controlled by it. Even if it seems, to you, to be too small or too crooked, a penis that can be controlled by you is more satisfying to any woman than an objectively "more handsome" penis that controls its master. In fact, the latter situation can lead to fears that have markedly negative effects on one's love life. So, enough already! In this book, you'll learn to familiarize yourself with your penis and its reactions. This knowledge will provide you with a boost of sexual energy.

In what ways exactly have you come to know your penis more closely? When you were a kid, it was all about long-distance pissing. Later, during puberty, you rediscovered your penis as the source of sexual pleasure. Back then, it was still fun to become more intimately acquainted with it. But that probably proved to be the last opportunity for intensive hands-on contact. You experimented, you conducted research – and finally, you hit on how it "works." You found that knowledge more than sufficient, and have hardly expanded it over the years.

But for anyone who wants to achieve real control, simply knowing how something works isn't enough. Maybe you were given a musical instrument when you were a kid – a recorder, or a harmonica. Sure, if you blow into it, sound will come out. But if you really want to master the instrument, then you have to learn how to use it correctly – not to mention practice. Are you not the musical type? Well, it's similar with a bicycle or a skateboard. Anyone can ride a bike. But there are people for whom bicycling becomes a passion, who can carry out mind-blowing stunts on a bike. The ability to simply ride isn't enough for them. It's that way with many things – and with your penis as well.

Not everyone wants to become a music virtuoso or an expert biker, but anyone who wants to have satisfying sex should at least master the most important sexual instrument. So, is that what you want? Then you've bought the right book – because a bike isn't what you'll be learning to ride here.

Many men feel the incentive to become a better lover. To that end, they buy books that tell them exactly how to satisfy a woman. They learn how to press all the right keys on the piano of the female body. That's to be welcomed, in any event.

But that all-important instrument – the penis – is for the most part neglected. Yes, it's important to become intimately acquainted with the female anatomy – but isn't it at least as important to get to know your own body, after all? That's exactly what you'll learn here.

The penis itself is not a muscle – otherwise, every fitness studio on the planet would be standing-room-only. There, men learn the art of bodybuilding. You might say that they pack quite a load of "dynamite" – but they neglect the "fuse." There is, however, one muscle that's essential for maintaining control of the penis. Training this muscle is the main goal! The good news is: You don't need any fitness studio or any other equipment to do it – and all it takes is just a few minutes a day.

The „PC-Muscle“

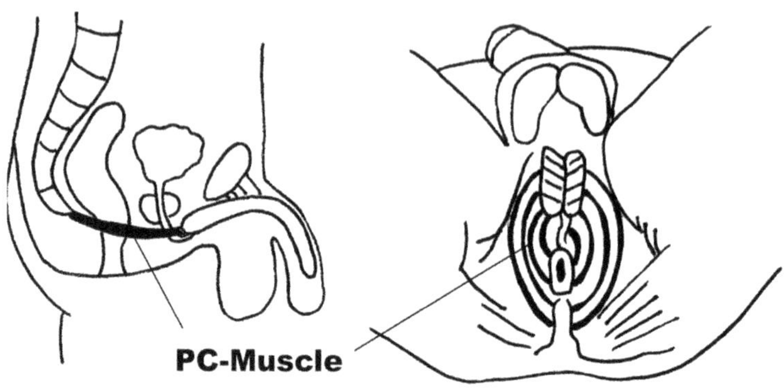

Illustration 4: Pubococcygeus-Muscle (PC-Muscle)

The most important muscle in this context is the pubococcygeus muscle. The pubo… what? Nevermind. From now on, we'll call it the PC-muscle.

This muscle exists in both men and women alike. Actually, it's a combination of several strands of muscle that are used for several activities. You know it most of all from controlling the flow of urine. When you're urinating, and you purposefully cut off the stream, or try to pee in spurts, then you're using precisely this muscle. You've certainly also tried to move your aroused member by tensing your muscles. That's also the PC-muscle. It too provides for the expulsion of semen during ejaculation. All told, it's a real jack-of-all-trades.

But still, it leads a shadowy existence, because it's capable of a lot more. It makes multiple orgasms possible, but only if it's correctly trained. A strong PC-muscle is the prerequisite for learning the MO-technique! Without it, nothing will work. Therefore, you'll also learn, in the exercise section, how you can strengthen it. Its importance can hardly be emphasized enough.

Have no fear – the training isn't all that hard. And the success it promises outweighs the effort expended by a long shot. Aside from the ability to have multiple orgasms, a strong PC-muscle brings with it further advantages as well. As a positive side-effect, well-trained pelvic muscles help prevent prostrate problems and bladder incontinence. These problems often develop in advanced age due to muscle weakness in the pelvic area.

Aside from that, the exercises will ensure a better overall level of health. Since the pelvic muscle structure provides the foundation for the rest of the body, it's of decisive importance for posture, as well as for the functioning of internal organs.

Potency Enhancement and Penis Enlargement as a Side Effect

Erectile difficulties can have numerous causes. Many of them can be corrected by training the PC-muscle! During muscle exercises, the entire surrounding tissue enjoys better blood circulation. A cleansing process takes place. In the process, residues are rinsed out. If the exercises are carried out in a deliberate manner, then one's erectile ability increases as a natural side effect. Patients report harder and bigger erections, conditioned by this training.

Often, impotence is also conditioned by insufficient use. The pelvic muscles of anyone who has sexual intercourse or masturbates rarely, or not at all, is often so weakened that it's not even enough to pump blood into the penis. In this case as well, PC-muscle training leads, step by step, to better circulation and, by the same token, to improved erectile ability.

The penis itself does not naturally become smaller or larger, without surgical intrusion. Nevertheless, if the pelvic muscles are lacking in strength, the penis is, over the years, "pulled" into the body. Externally, this process may be observed as an apparent shrinking. It's especially prevalent among men who are rarely sexually active. Through PC-muscle training, the pelvic muscles are strengthened, and the penis is once again "pressed" outwards. This leads to an optical penis enlargement. As mentioned above, the size and hardness of the erections are also increased by flexible and well-trained pelvic muscles. Later, you'll learn yet another exercise that is aimed especially at enlarging the penis.

But the most important aspect this newly-won "penis power" brings with it is an increased feeling of self-worth. Anyone who has control over his pelvic muscles, and thus over his penis – and knows it – does not need to worry any more about whether or not "it" will "play along." He enters the bedroom with the positive awareness of his own abilities, and thus frees himself from all fears and mental barriers, which are the most common reasons for erectile difficulties.

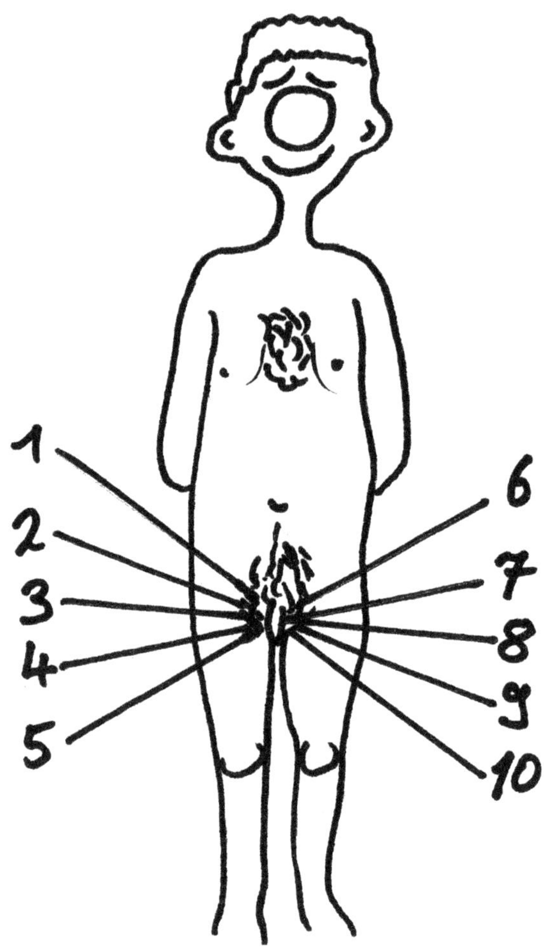

Illustration 5: The erogenous zones of the man

Erogenous Zones

Yeah, that's often the way it feels. Indeed, for the majority of men, everything revolves around the penis. But we too have erogenous zones that are often neglected, and which remain undiscovered by most men for their entire lives. Here, it's well worth it to experiment a bit with your own body.

I'll name for you a few spots on the body that you certainly know of, and others that may be completely new to you. Perhaps you've neglected those you know of, because they don't arouse you as powerfully as stimulation of the penis. On the one hand, men are naturally different, and any one of these spots may bring more arousal to one man than to another. Nevertheless, you should also know that different spots only become active at a certain level of arousal. You'll learn more about arousal level later.

It's also well worth it to give some thought to this fact, and bring these various spots into play during self-arousal, as well as during love-making. Then you'll see which ones bring you pleasure and which ones don't really work for you.

Some of the spots may provide you with a peculiar, unique feeling of orgasm with which you were previously unacquainted. In any case, through the involvement of several erogenous zones, sex becomes a multi-sensoral experience that envelops the entire body.

Let's embark on a voyage of discovery across, and into, your body.

The Nipples

Most men probably attribute a secondary significance to their own nipples. Many more are a lot more fixated on female breasts. With men, as with women, the potential for arousal of the nipples differs from person to person. For some, all it may take is a slight touch to send arousal into orbit. Others need firm stimulation, up to and including pinching and biting. But for most, it's the case that the intensity of the touch is perceived differently at different levels of arousal.

Many men discover that the nerves in the nipples must be "activated" through regular stimulation. So it's worth it to get the nipples involved in love-making. Your partner can do this by stroking, kissing, or tender pinching and nibbling. When pleasuring yourself, you can use your free hand to stimulate, along with your penis, other erogenous zones as well – in this case, the nipples.

Especially if the nipples haven't been on the sexual menu up to now, then they're just begging to have special attention paid to them during stimulation. Anyone who thinks, during his partner's tender nipple-kisses, "OK, great… when will she finally go downstairs?" is probably missing something. It's better to explain to your partner that she should vary the manner of touching, and to concentrate on the reactions of your own body. Only this will make it possible to recognize the fact that you're reaping enjoyment, and to increase it. In any case, it's always worth it to pay attention to your partner's touches, because these often reveal to you the ways in which she herself would most like to be touched. If things are different for you, then tell her so.

If your nipples prove not to be too arousing for you, even after several attempts, then don't worry about it. At any rate, you've gotten to know your body better. But you should at least know what you're turning down… otherwise, perhaps, you'll miss out on a surprise.

The Anus

The anus is a highly erogenous zone, since there are a great deal of nerve endings in this region. Many men, both homo- and heterosexual, value this manner of stimulation as being extremely pleasurable. And yet there are many men who never come to know this sexual potential. It is a taboo zone that is often viewed as dirty or degenerate. Many men even have a feeling of homophobia and, along with it, fear of being considered gay, or even becoming gay, if they begin to probe this topic.

But there's no reason for that. Homosexuality is a sexual orientation, independent of anal sensitivity and sexual practices. And this erogenous zone is only dirty if hygiene is neglected. In order to have a truly clean feeling, you can inspect this area in the shower. A bit of lubricant is also helpful.

The stimulation possibilities are varied: external stroking and rubbing, playing around with fingers or a dildo, licking and kissing. Anything that pleases is allowed. Try to be open and eager to experiment, and don't reject something you don't know. If you don't like it, you can always stop. And if you do, you will have discovered an important erogenous zone.

The Prostate

In contrast to the penis, nipples and anus, the prostate is an erogenous zone that is not visible from without. This internal gland has the approximate size and shape of a chestnut, but the arousal potential of a watermelon. I don't mean to attribute any sexual significance to the watermelon as such, although I once heard of an island tribe that… well, maybe some other time.

Most men know the prostate only from those uncomfortable examinations at the doctor's, which help to provide early detection of much-feared prostate cancer. Through the exercises described in this book, you'll prevent prostate problems! The exercises for training the PC-muscle strengthen the entire pelvic muscle structure, and massage the prostate, providing it with good blood circulation and good health.

A brief word about the function and structure of the prostate: most of the ejaculate expelled during orgasm is produced in the prostate. The sperm cells, mind you, originate in the testicles. The prostate consists of approximately 40 individual glands, which are surrounded by a binding tissue and embedded inside a muscle. During ejaculation, the muscle pushes the secretion through the spermatic duct, which flows into the urethra. The urethra runs through the middle of the prostate. That's the most important information, in short. Let's get to the pleasure you stand to gain.

If the prostate is involved in love-making, it will be able to develop its orgasmic potential. And indeed, the prostate can even be compared with a woman's G-spot. Perry, Kahn and Whipple, in their publication entitled "The G-Spot," arrived at the result that the prostate, alongside the penis, can unleash a special kind of orgasm. The difference might be said to be comparable to the female distinction between clitoral and vaginal orgasm.

It should be noted that the prostate – as with a woman's G-spot – only becomes active as a pleasure spot once a certain level of arousal is reached. That's why you don't get off during those doctor's examinations.

How can you tap into these sexual pleasures?

The prostate can best be reached if you're lying on your back – either with your legs spread and set up, or with your knees tucked against your chest. Now, either your partner or yourself can penetrate the anus by about 1,5 inches, and search for the "chestnut." Vary the manner and pressure of your touch (stroking, knocking, pressing). Take care that your fingernails are trimmed, and that you use an oil-based, or, better yet, water-based lubricant.

If you aren't in the mood for anal penetration, you can also stimulate the perineum, just in front of the anus, by applying moderate to strong pressure – and massaging, with the fingertips, using a circular motion.

You'll derive particular enjoyment if your partner combines prostate stimulation with oral pleasure. Or, as the publisher of Hustler, Larry Flint, said: "A blow job, a finger in my ass, and a good cigar to go with it – for me, that's paradise."

The Perineum

The perineum's problem is that it's located between the two prime attractions, the penis and the anus – for that reason, no one gives it any attention. But before we start to pity it, let's rather examine this important region more thoroughly. According to the Tao, this is where the "point of a million gold coins" or "Jen-Mo-point" is located. This point isn't only an erogenous zone, but can also be enlisted in ejaculation control. Therefore, this point will be dealt with later, along with the techniques.

As an erogenous zone, you can touch the area from the bottom of the shaft of your penis all the way to your anus, with your fingertips. Vary the pressure and the manner of movement, and find out what's the most fun for you.

The Testicles

One more short joke, to loosen things up a bit:

At a high-society ball, a couple is dancing. She says to him: "Sir, your shop is open for business!" He: "It's embarrassing for me to look down. Can you tell me if the shopkeeper is poking his head out?" She (after an examining glance): "No, just the two clerks..."

OK, that didn't come out so well. But we're now concerned precisely with these clerks. As with the "point of a million gold coins," the testicles can play a role in ejaculation control.

But they too are an erogenous zone. The "clerks" are especially happy when they're stroked or fondled – best of all, with soft female lips. If they're in the mood, then they derive great fun from movement, such as "pulling the rope" or "the tickle." The only thing they don't like is "the sack race."

Enough with the joking around... let's get on the ball!

Conclusion

We're now at the end of our journey of discovery, and perhaps you've gained an interesting stimulus or two to make use of more of your body during love-making than just your penis.

These erogenous zones were a brief supplement to our real topic: multiple orgasms. For that, the PC-muscle, which you've just gotten to know, is the decisive factor.

No Strong PC-Muscle – No Multiple Orgasm!

The training described later is important, and necessary, in order to achieve control over your penis. The training itself is simple, and just a few minutes per day will be more than sufficient. But it's important that it be carried out in a thorough manner. The advantages described above, which strong pelvic muscles bring, should be motivation enough.

In this chapter, you've discovered the potential that your penis and PC-muscle can offer. Now it's time to get down to business. First, we'll concern ourselves with your PC-muscle, and give you "PC-power."

Then you'll learn how your tools can be used to ensure that nothing else stands in the way of your multi-orgasm abilities.

Now you'll learn the MO-technique. Ready?

Then read further.

5. The Road to Mastery

You've already learned how it's possible, even as a man, to achieve multiple orgasms. With that, you've attained the **knowledge**. Now you need to learn the **ability** as well. I'll show you exercises that will allow you, with and without your partner, to achieve the desired success in the most efficient manner possible, and with minimal effort. You can do many of the exercises "on the side." You don't need any accessories! You can do the exercises as described, and they'll bring you success. On the other hand, you might arrive, during your training, at other ideas or tricks that work well for you. Great! Whatever works for you is correct! Experiment, and let yourself be inspired by the exercises. If you've discovered a path that you especially like, then I'd love to hear about it! (feedback@mannkann.com). That goes as well for constructive criticism of the exercises described.

During my research on this topic, I encountered the fact that Chinese Tao-masters often instructed their students in the secret techniques for years on end. That led me to the idea of a pictorial structure for the exercises. As a metaphor for the levels of the exercises, I've chosen the levels of accomplishment of Japanese karate: The colored belt ranking system. So you'll begin as a beginner, with a white belt, and work your way step by step through the various colors, all the way to the black belt. This symbolizes mastery of the MO-technique (the multi-orgasm technique).

Because this book is directed at men, and many men have already had contact with Asian martial arts, this concept may already be familiar to you. But it doesn't matter if you've never heard anything about the belt system. The steps are numbered, and you can simply go through them in order. The belt colors symbolize the level of accomplishment at which you now find yourself. In this way, you'll get a good overview of your progress.

If you then believe that you're ready for the next belt, write me an e-mail; we'll arrange a meeting, and you can carry out the grading examination in front of me.

That was a joke, of course, because here's the good news: the "belt-examinations" aren't carried out officially, nor do they last as long as with karate, where several months can separate the various tests. You'll do the tests at your own pace. If you think you've come far enough, you can move on to the next step.

Many men have their first multi-orgasmic experiences after just 1-2 weeks. The majority require between 3-6 months to become multi-orgasmic. So don't worry if it takes a bit longer. If you really make an effort to attain this ability, then your success is assured!

I hope that none of this sounds to you like work and effort. The "exercises" are more of a practical journey of discovery through your sexual abilities. You'll get to know your body better, use it more efficiently, and have a lot of fun doing it – guaranteed.

The Training – Step By Step To Success

Here we go! Are you excited yet, and fully motivated? Great – because the more enthusiasm you have for the topic, the greater success you'll have in learning.

Still, it's important to go through the levels of accomplishment in order, and not to skip any. If you do so, you'll only be fooling yourself, and in the end, things will only take longer. The exercise program is directed at optimal learning success, and every single step has a particular sense.

For every belt, you'll find solo as well as partner exercises. And since we're oriented towards karate, the solo exercises are called "kata," and the partner exercises are called "kumite." It might sound new to you now, but you'll get used to it quickly, and it makes the entire system more authentic. When we come to it, we'll also introduce the concept of "dojo," which literally means "the place for practicing the path." What is meant is a training hall in which the martial arts are practiced – in our case, the bedroom. So the sentence, "I'm going to the dojo to do some kata training," takes on a whole new meaning.

But back to the solo and partner exercises – that is, kata and kumite. To attain each belt, you only need to do one of the two.

You can decide for yourself whether you prefer to practice alone, or would prefer to do a certain exercise with your partner. The variant that's more suitable is presented first. But both are equally valuable for reaching your learning goal. If you'd like, of course, you can also try both variants. Perhaps you'd like to practice alone first, before you give what you've learned a try with your partner. Wonderful. Use the exercises in whatever way makes you happiest.

Just take care to do at least one exercise for every belt, and to stick to the order of the training plan. Then you'll attain your black belt in "penis karate" in no time.

Exercise Preparation

Before every effective training, a sensible preparation takes place. Whether it's stretching or checking the equipment just depends on the kind of sport. In our case, preparation consists of creating an atmosphere conducive to exercise.

Here, you'll find a couple of general suggestions that will allow you to be able to carry out your exercises in a relaxed environment. The following two sections delve briefly into the particularities of solo and partner exercises.

It's important, first of all, to take time out for yourself. Free yourself from the everyday, so that you can concentrate for 30-60 minutes (according to the given exercise) completely on your body, your arousal, and your learning goal. Turn off the mobile phone, so that you won't be disturbed. Then your "training" will become a relaxed, pleasurable experience, and you'll have a load of fun.

Further, it's recommended that you find a comfortable environment that stimulates all of your senses. Create a relaxed sound backdrop with quiet music, and use perfume oils or incense-sticks to create an air that excites you. Keep a couple of treats ready at hand (for example, fruit, wine or chocolate), so you'll be able to have a bite during the process. The room should be at a comfortable temperature.

This multi-sensoral surrounding makes the training not only more pleasant, but also more effective, since all the senses are appealed to. Sound, smell, taste… and we're about to get to touch. Thereby, several areas of the brain are stimulated, which increases your learning success. This is an important tip for other learning situations as well!

Regardless of whether you're practicing alone or with a partner, it's recommended to have a lubricant close at hand. Oil works, but better yet is an oil-free, water- or silicone-based lubricating gel. I recommend the product "Pjur," which you can buy in any sex shop, in black bottles of various sizes. It's not cheap, but the very smallest amounts of it are sufficient; besides, it also works great for massage. Since it doesn't contain oil, it doesn't affect latex condoms.

Summary:

- Take some time out for yourself (mobile phone off!).
- Put on some relaxing music.
- Create a pleasant atmosphere.
- Have some refreshments ready.
- Use a lubricant.

Solo Exercises – Kata

"Do-it-yourself." Maybe you don't have a committed partner at the moment, or maybe you'd prefer to practice alone, in order to surprise your wife or girlfriend with your multi-orgasmic abilities. You can learn the MO-technique without getting a partner involved.

Even if you're practicing alone, the suggestions for creating a comfortable atmosphere are still valid. I recommend that you use a lubricant, since you'll be handling your pleasure piston for a fair amount of time. And we certainly don't want you to get blisters.

From now on, the solo practices will be called "kata." The name is japanese, and describes a series of particular karate techniques that are practiced alone – much like shadow boxing.

But your dojo is the living room or bedroom. You can do your exercises on a comfortable chair, a couch, or in bed. There's no dress code, since you'll be either naked, or very lightly clothed.

Special details for the particular exercises will be addressed in the corresponding descriptions..

Partner Exercises – Kumite

Partner exercises mean double the fun. Here you'll be sharing your satisfaction and pleasure with your partner, which will bring a new depth to your relationship. The two of you will learn to pay attention to each other's signals, and, thereby, get to know each other better. The result is a relaxed and intimate communication during love-making, and a profound sense of trust.

Take the exercises as a road map for an exciting voyage of discovery through the body and the arousal of your partner. Read through the description together beforehand, and discuss the individual points, so that no questions remain open.

Agree upon a couple of signs so that you'll be able to make yourself understood even without words. During many exercises, your partner will have to stop the stimulation at the right moment. For this, hand signs will work, for example, such as a raised hand or a cutting movement. Of course, you can also simply say "stop."

As a man, I'd advise you to pay attention to what your partner does when she wants to arouse you. Even when it's not exactly what works best for you, it's often a sign of what she wants herself. After the exercise, I recommend that you give each other mutual feedback. A discussion after the fact greatly elevates your learning success. Treat each other lovingly and respectfully, and be patient. Everything is allowed, as long as it's fun for both of you. The important thing is that the mood be relaxed and free from pressure of any kind.

Here's another bit of advice for all women. You can also use the exercises to your own benefit. Through them, you'll get to know your own stimulation better, and learn how to control it. This will also make it easier for you to experience multiple orgasms.

Safer Sex

You've certainly heard it a thousand times already, but this is, of course, the place for a tip concerning safer sex.

If you tend to have contact with frequently changing partners, I advise you to use condoms. You can catch all kinds of illnesses from sexual activity. Of course, you can also use condoms as a means of birth control in a committed relationship.

The MO-technique makes safe sex even "safer." Following ejaculation, a vacuum develops in the urethra, which can draw the bodily fluids of your partner into the penis. If ejaculation is avoided, no vacuum develops in the urethra. Thus, less bodily fluid is exchanged, which minimizes the communication of pathogens. Still, this is just an additional benefit, which makes condoms still necessary for protection and as a means of birth control.

The important thing is that you can learn the MO-technique with condoms as well, and there's no reason to do without them during the exercises.

Using a Condom

If you're using a condom, then you've surely already had some experience with them. But regardless of whether you're a rubber-rookie or an expert rubberchutist, maybe there are a couple of tips here for you.

Many men have problems with the instructions that are included. Above all, this technique just does not work on larger models.

Here's a technique that works on any size:

- Take the rolled-up condom between the thumb and index finger of both hands, with the reservoir facing upwards.

- Now, unroll approximately a third of the condom, using the index finger, middle finger, and thumb.

- Now, stick the index and middle fingers of both hands into the unrolled portion of the condom.

- Now, you can stretch the condom and pull it over the penis.

- Let your fingertips remain inside the condom, in order to carefully unroll the remainder. When your fingers are still inside the condom, you can, with further stretching and pulling, roll it out all the way to the bottom.

It's important that the condom covers the entire penis, and that there be a bit of room at the top (the reservoir). If you use condoms, I especially recommend that you use a water- or silicone-based lubricant that does not attack the latex.

After sexual intercourse, you should pull out your still-erect member while holding the condom in place with your fingers, to make sure it doesn't slip off.

1. The White Belt

Now we're finally here. The training is beginning, and with it, your path towards the multiple orgasm. The goal of this stage of the exercises is to locate the PC-muscle. It's the foundation upon which the following exercises are built. In karate, the pendant would be the correct position necessary to ensure a clean execution of the techniques.

You'll also learn something about your breathing, which can help you to control your body. This exercise too is the basis for later exercises, during which you can influence your arousal with the help of breathing.

But first we have to deal with the most important weapon in the "struggle" for the multiple orgasm: the PC-muscle.

Finding the PC-Muscle

Before you can learn to apply the PC-muscle in a targeted fashion, you must first learn to find it in your body. To locate the PC-muscle, it's not necessary to have an erection.

Since several muscle groups lie close to one another in the pelvic region, it's important to isolate the PC-muscle. Here are two excercises to find it.

Kata: The Dam

The simplest way to find the PC-muscle is by cutting off the stream while urinating. This is precisely the muscle you're looking for. Notice how it feels when you flex it. Try to halt the stream several times, and, in so doing, to pee in spurts. Only flex the muscle you need for this, and take care to leave the surrounding regions loose – especially the stomach and buttock muscles. Flex the PC-muscle a few more times, as soon as you're done.

If you can locate the muscle in this way, the exercise is over for you. If you don't need to use the restroom at the moment, or want to make sure you found the right muscle, then do the following exercise.

Kata: Catch the Worm

This exercise is simplest when you're naked, but it also works, in the case of necessity, when clothed. Here's a tip: do the exercise in the bathroom – after showering, for example.

1. Get yourself situated.
2. Place two fingers beneath the testicles.
3. Try, in a targeted fashion, to raise your testicles.
4. If you can sense with your fingers how the testicles rise a bit, then you've got the right muscle.

Here too, it's important to flex in isolation, and to purposefully leave the surrounding pelvic region loose.

Now you should know where the muscle is located, and how it feels to flex it.

Breathing

Breathing is an important instrument of control over our body. In sports as well as in medicine, breathing is used in order to obtain certain effects.

Breathing is connected with the heart rate – and vice versa. With physical exertion, or in stressful situations, the pulse and the breathing become automatically shallower. If we force ourselves to breathe more calmly and more deeply, then our pulse drops. So, by way of breathing, we can consciously affect our heart rate.

Orgasm is defined by, among other things, a rise of the pulse rate. Our breathing as well becomes shallower and faster when we are aroused. In this context, shallower refers to a breathing that occurs mostly in the chest.

Our goal, then, is to learn a deep and calm stomach and diaphragm breathing, with the help of which we can bridle the wild horse of arousal. This technique will come into use in a later chapter. Here, what we want is to develop a feel for correct breathing.

With deep breathing, more air is exchanged, and the blood can be better provided with oxygen. This promotes both physical and spiritual activity. Unfortunately, we often unlearn this healthy manner of breathing through fear or stress. In both cases, breathing is confined to the upper thorax – but both can be positively influenced by deep breathing. If you go through the exercise regularly, your body will soon learn again how to breathe correctly unconsciously – even in sleep.

Kata: A Valley Wind

During this exercise, a fresh wind should flow into the deepest valleys of your lungs.

1. Sit upright in a chair. Lay one hand softly on your stomach.
2. Breath in calmly through the nose, until you notice that your stomach has expanded.
3. Imagine your upper body as a hollow space, and visualize how the air flows into it and fills it from within, until the abdominal wall is pressed outwards.
4. When you exhale, all of the air is pushed out of this hollow space. You can support this if you pull back your stomach when exhaling. Exhale through the mouth.
5. Breath out until you can't exhale any further.
6. Repeat steps 3 through 5 at least 10 times.

The important thing during this exercise is not to try to press the air out in a constrained and tensed-up fashion. Listen to your own body, and make a conscious effort to support its natural breathing with calm and intensive power.

2. The Yellow Belt

Well, that was easy, wasn't it? But let's not have any false hopes. Not all the belts are this easy to earn. Even the next one will be more difficult. Now that you've located the PC-muscle with the help of the previous exercise, your task is to train it.

An Important Bit of Advice:

I've already told you that you should first complete one step before you make an attempt at the next belt. Here, there's one exception. "The exception proves the rule." Ha, you must be kidding! I've always wanted to attack this thoughtless proverb in a book. Exceptions don't prove any rule – they disprove them. That's why they're called exceptions. No exception has ever proven a rule. Think that over, and the next time someone uses this saying, be a smart-ass – just like I'm being right now! Well, that just had to come out here. Let's get back to the topic.

The exception is that you can proceed directly with the orange belt as soon as you've learned the PC-muscle training. You should continue practicing the exercises for increasing the strength of your PC-muscle throughout the entire program. From the blue belt on, in any case, you'll require a well-trained PC-muscle.

One more time, as a reminder: stay on the ball! It takes just a few minutes per day, and if you do the exercises regularly, you'll have made considerable progress after just three weeks.

PC-Muscel-Training

Like a karate fighter who steels his body, from this moment on, you'll be training your PC-muscle. But instead of attacking a sandbag with jabs and kicks, this training occurs within your body – with PC-jabs and PC-kicks.

These names should help you to distinguish between the exercises, since the power of the exercises is comparable to short, quick jabs and slow, powerful kicks.

In contrast to the other exercises, you have no choice in this case. It is important to master both variants in order to optimally build up the PC-muscle. With these two exercises, you'll also increase the endurance and the maximum power of the PC-muscle. A karate fighter must also train himself in arm and leg techniques. Then, he is optimally prepared should a battle ensue. In exactly the same way, you'll be prepared should a "mattress battle" come.

The good news is that the PC-muscle responds quite rapidly to training. Nevertheless, it's true that "slow and steady wins the race."

A clichéd bit of wisdom, I know. But the truth it contains still holds, especially when it comes to training the PC-muscle. All the exercises will only lead to the desired result if you do them **regularly**. It's like training in a gym. Since we're dealing with a muscle, it needs regular exercises in order to build itself up. The advantage is that one doesn't need any gym, and no additional equipment. I'll explain exercises to you that you can do at any time. In the line at the supermarket, driving your car, at the movie theater, at work, or at the university. Just keep in mind – it's worth the effort!

Once the muscle is built up, you simply need to do "maintenance" exercises. In the beginning, the training is perhaps a bit unusual and demanding, but the more you train, the easier the exercises will seem to you.

You yourself determine your learning success; the more you train, the sooner you'll reach your goal!

PC-Jabs:

1. Flex your PC-muscle, briefly and powerfully (for a maximum of 1 second).
2. Relax the muscle again.
3. Repeat the exercise 20 times.

You should do this exercise three times daily for a period of at least three weeks. The practical thing about this exercise is that you can really do it everywhere – the possibilities are endless. The only problem is that one rarely thinks about it. A couple of helpful tips and tricks for this exercise can be found later in this chapter.

The exercise is – like most exercises of this sort – a modification of the Kegel exercises. The gynecologist Arnold Kegel developed the exercises in the 40s for pregnant women. They helped with bladder control and made it easier to give birth. As a positive side effect, the women reported increased desire and more intense orgasms.

PC-Kicks:

1. Flex the PC-muscle slowly (increasing over a period of three seconds), and hold the tension for five seconds. Exhale while flexing the muscle.
2. Relax the muscle again slowly and inhale.
3. Report the exercise 20 times.

You should do this exercise three times per day – best of all, in the morning when you wake up, while you're still lying in bed. Then, maybe, on the way to work, or in the line at the supermarket. And one more time in the evening – for example, while watching television.

It may be that this exercise will seem downright difficult to you in the beginning. Perhaps your muscle will become tired after just 2 or 3 flexes. No problem! Try to progress slowly until you can manage 20 repetitions at a time – that is, 60 total per day. If you're in good shape, and you think yourself capable of more, then you can easily do 100 per day. The more you do, the more quickly you'll have success. But make sure that you don't overexert yourself in the beginning.

Important:

The important thing with this exercise is to flex the PC-muscle in as isolated a manner as possible. Try to breath evenly, and not to flex your stomach muscles.

If it turns out to be hard for you to keep your stomach muscles loose, you can also do a couple of sit-ups before the exercise, in order to "power out" your stomach muscles. If you exhaust these muscles beforehand, they won't get in your way anymore during your PC-muscle training. The positive side effect is that, aside from your PC-power, you'll also get smashing six pack abs.

Stop the Stream

This exercise, which I developed myself, will show you how you can train even while urinating. The advantage is that in this way you'll automatically train regularly, once you've gotten used to it. Resolve to urinate in this manner regularly, from this moment on.

1. At first, press powerfully, several times, in spurts.
2. Stop the stream, and hold it for the duration of a single breath.
3. Repeat steps 1 and 2 two to three times.

This exercise too has a practical advantage that I've really learned to value. Earlier, it was impossible for me to stop the stream once it had been unleashed, and subsequently to control the need to urinate. That really became a problem when I was forced, during a traffic jam, to piss into a bottle, because otherwise my bladder would have burst. Unfortunately, the bottle wasn't big enough… you can imagine the rest. But with a strong PC-muscle, you'll be able to stop your stream at any time, close the bottle and button your pants, and, after a short while, get rid of the need to urinate – an ability that can spare you many embarrassing situations.

Tips & Tricks

Here are a few tips and tricks that have proven themselves in training:

General Tips

- Don't overdo your training – especially when you're just getting started. When this muscle gets sore it can be quite unpleasant.

- Always try to flex the muscle in a targeted fashion. Take care not to flex the entire pelvic muscle structure and/or the stomach muscles along with it. If necessary, tire out the stomach muscles beforehand with sit-ups.

- Pay attention to your breathing. Don't hold your breath during the exercises, but continue breathing calmly and deeply.

- Progress slowly. Especially if your penis is a bit out of practice, don't wear it out right away with the entire training workload. Start out with a few repetitions, and increase them in a way that is comfortable for your body.

Don't give up! Always keep your goal in sight. It's worth it!

Special Tricks for Practice

- Train whenever the thought occurs to you – while driving, at the movie theater, at work, while talking on the telephone, during lectures, at the supermarket, in bed, in an airplane…

- A small post-it note, with the mysterious letters "PC," can serve as a reminder ¬ on the dashboard of your car, on the refrigerator, on the telephone, or on the television.

- If you spend a lot of time driving, you can also use objects on the side of the road as short targets for your PC-training. Try, for example, to keep your PC-muscle flexed until you drive past that sign 100 meters in the distance. In this way, you create for yourself a finish line that you're expected to attain.

- You can, for example, give a PC-jab to every attractive woman who crosses your path. Whenever you notice a woman, flex your PC-muscle and keep it flexed for as long as you look at the woman. If you can't take it any more, you'll have to look away. This exercise is a lot of fun, and is a good motivator.

- Always train while urinating – to build up the muscle, and, later, to maintain it.

- Keep records of your training. This is an important bit of advice that can really increase your motivation. You can, for example, put dashes or circles in your calendar, or on the refrigerator. You can also enter circles in the calendar that stand for training sessions remaining to be done; for example, a circle in the morning, mid-day, and evening, in which you can then enter the number of the repetitions you've done. Then, you'll not only be reminded to do your training, but you'll also have an overview of the progress you've made.

3. The Orange Belt

Welcome to the level of the orange belt, and congratulations! From this point on, the training will become significantly more erotic! And finally, you can, in addition, get your partner involved as well, who, perhaps, is already waiting impatiently. But even without a partner, we're now getting to significantly more enjoyable exercises. That's a promise!

In order to reap the greatest possible amount of physical pleasure, we must dedicate ourselves to our own body. Only if we know the various possibilities for increasing pleasure can we reach erotic heights – with or without a partner. Therefore, this chapter is aimed at sensual touching.

Sensual Touching

In our fast-paced day, we all look for quick satisfaction. If we're hungry, then we scarf down a burger, and if we're aroused, then we have a quickie, or play a round of pocket billiards. As satisfying as fast food may sometimes be, it's also important to be properly nourished. Fresh spices and ingredients of a higher quality require a bit more time during preparation to become a culinary delight. The satisfaction that comes as a result is, however, incomparably greater than the one promised by a burger. If we're already too used to fast food or to plain home cooking, then our taste buds need a little practice in order to become sensitive to more nuanced pleasures.

The exercises for sensual touching do exactly that for the sense of touch. Above and beyond that tried-and-true burger, your senses should be sharpened for strange delicacies – in this case, unaccustomed touches.

In our society, given the image of the "tough guy," it's considered sissy to sensitize and spoil the senses. But this kind of satisfaction is every bit as manly as excruciating pain – only a lot more pleasant.

We aren't dealing in these exercises with arousal. We'll deal with with that when we come to the green belt. Here, enjoyment is front and center. This exercise is especially fun with a partner, and for this reason, the partner exercise (kumite) is introduced first.

Kumite - A Breath of Air

For this partner exercise, the two of you should take a good hour's worth of time. It will be a thrilling hour, that much I can assure you! Good thing we're not practicing karate here, since one person gives while the other receives. You can breathe a sigh of relief, knowing that we're dealing with details of caresses, and not karate chops.

Basically, one of the partners is the active party (the giver), while the other remains passive (the recipient), surrendering completely to the touches. After 20 minutes, places are swapped, so that both partners get their money's worth, and get to know both sides.

During this exercise, you should do without music, so that the two of you can concentrate completely on the touches. I suggest you use your bedroom as your dojo. Make things comfortable for yourselves on the bed, where the recipient should first lie on his or her stomach. Once the recipient has found a comfortable position, he should maintain it until the next step. You can use oil or lubricant gel, as much as you want, but it also works without it.

The giver begins with slow, sensual touches, which should include the entire body. From a soft pressure with the fingertips on the head, to long, stroking motions down the legs. You can also take the name of the exercise literally and let a breath of air pass over the body. But please use your mouth for that, and not another orifice of your body. When the backside has been provided for, the recipient should lie on his back, with slightly spread legs; find a comfortable position, and maintain it.

Both partners concentrate completely and totally on the touches, and the sensations that they unleash. The recipient should close his eyes and direct his concentration completely on that spot where the touching is taking place. Moreover, the body should be completely relaxed. If the giver notices that the recipient's attention is waning, or that the body is tensing up, he or she should give a relaxation signal agreed upon beforehand. This could be, for example, a soft knocking or pressing. If the recipient notices that his concentration is wandering – either on its own, or due to the partner's signal – he should direct his attention once again to the place where the touching is occurring. But the giver as well should concentrate fully on the touches. He or she can enjoy the view that presents itself, and gain an awareness of how the contact feels.

Basically, the exploration should proceed from the outside inwards. Once you're done with the head, face, hands, feet, arms, legs, breast, and stomach, you can get started with a gentle massage of the genitals. I must stress once again that this exercise has nothing to do with an orgasm. It's OK if you get an erection, but that's not the goal. Be very clear that you won't put it to use, and no unpleasant sense of pressure will arise. In this exercise, as they say, the path itself is the destination.

There are a few tips as to how one should touch a woman. The touches should be carried out in ever-narrowing circles, around particularly sensitive areas. Thus, you can, for example, first make broad circles around the breast, before making your way, with stroking motions, to the nipples.

Since the recipient keeps his or her eyes closed, a shiver may caused if there is an unexpectedly long interval between particular touches. If, for example, you move over the collarbone for 1-3 seconds, and then jump to the inner side of the thigh, this is extremely stimulating for most women. Use this technique as a variation, but don't go overboard.

Furthermore, many women like it when the fingers glide over the hollow of the knee and the elbow, like a breath of air. Other women, on the contrary, feel this to be unpleasantly ticklish. But the exercise is constructed precisely in order to get to the bottom of what pleases you and your partner the most.

During the exercise, you can completely explore your partner – from the inside as well. Pay attention to the other's signals, so that you notice if a touch is unpleasant. Be soft and tender, and pay attention to your own feelings, both as the recipient and as the giver. You should only speak, during the entire exercise, if something is unpleasant for you.

If the two of you have played both roles, and have both properly spoiled each other, then the exercise is over. What you do to each other now is between the two of you; I have no desire to even hear about it. OK, actually, I'd be quite interested…

The Key Points, At a Glance

- Each partner is a giver once, and a recipient once.
- Take time for yourselves, and create a pleasant atmosphere – preferably, for this exercise, without music.
- Oil is helpful, but not necessary.
- Find a comfortable position, and stick with it. Relax.
- Direct your attention fully towards the point where the touching is occurring – both as recipient and as giver.
- Agree on a sign (a soft knocking), in case the recipient unconsciously begins to tense up.
- Stroke, massage, caress – working your way from the outside in.
- Take enough time for an extensive genital massage.
- Pay attention to the fullness of your sensations that arise during stimulation.
- An erection is OK, but is not required.
- Avoid pressure or having any set expectations.
- Only speak if something becomes unpleasant.
- Enjoy the touches, and discover the feelings that arise during them.

.

Kata - A Voyage of Discovery

Even without a partner, you can still embark on a voyage of discovery – in this case, across your own body. Chill out for thirty minutes, and make yourself comfortable. Sit in a comfortable chair or on the couch, or lie in bed. You don't need clothes for this exercise, so get rid of them. An oil or lubricant is, on the contrary, an advantage, so if you have some handy, now's the right moment to grab it.

When you're setting out on the voyage of discovery, don't start out right away at the Leaning Tower of Pisa. Instead, work your way down from the mountaintops over the lowlands (or the hill, according to your build). When you make your way out of the forest, you'll discover that, instead of Pisa, you've landed in Paris, and the Eiffel Tower is standing right in front of you.

If you're no world traveler, I'll summarize all of that one again, without metaphors: Don't rush to grab your penis right away, but instead stroke, pinch, and scratch yourself in other places first. Play with your nipples, stroke across the inner side of your thigh, and feel your stomach, and your breathing. Take the time to discover your body. So, have you gotten downright randy over yourself? In that case, now you can grab it.

Hey, not so rough! Remember: This is an exercise for sensual touch. So let go of your accustomed stranglehold, and first stroke yourself around the penis. Softly massage your scrotum while varying the pressure, so that you'll learn what you like best.

Variation is also called for when you make your way to the penis. The technique that has "worked" for you up to now is the only one that you may not use now. Instead, you should break out of your old rut, and treat it to some touches of a completely new kind. Stroke the entire penis. Scratch it, with soft pressure, along the shaft. Take it firmly in hand and press, for as long as it's comfortable. Experiment and discover new sources of pleasure that you can derive from your own body. The change of pace will definitely be good for the big guy. With oil, this part of the exercise is especially pleasant, since the hands glide better over the sensitive skin. In case of necessity, even a simple household oil, such as, for example, sunflower oil, will work. While your active hand stimulates the penis, you can continue your expedition with the other hand.

As the next important zone, you should dedicate yourself to the area between the anus and the testicles. This is where the "point of a million gold coins" is located, which you can stimulate with soft, circular movements. If you'd like, and have a lubricant handy, then you can get the anus involved too. You can either make circles around it, with varying pressure, or insert a finger. Several nerve endings lie in this area, which is why it is especially sensitive to the touch. Be sure your fingernails are trimmed, and that you use plenty of lubricant.

After that, you can sweep through the area between the anus and the base of the penis, with varying pressure. Here, aside from the "Jen-Mo-point," are further "hot spots" that only become active once you've passed a certain level of arousal. Therefore, you should return to places you've already knocked off, as your arousal rises. Many points are unpleasant at first, and only unfold with growing excitement. Observe how you react to the touches. Does your excitement increase more at certain places than at others? Get to know yourself better in this exercise.

Excitement itself, however, isn't the goal of this exercise, but merely the means to an end. An erection is therefore not necessary for the exercise. Naturally, I understand completely if you get one. Pay attention to the multifaceted sensations that overcome you, and that come along with arousal. What unleashes it? How does it feel? You should ask yourself these questions in order to get the most out of this exercise.

When you're ready to end the exploration, and are of the opinion that an orgasm would do you good now, then I'm the last person to hold you back. If you're ready to stop now, that's fine too, because an orgasm isn't necessary to fulfill the goal of the exercise.

The Key Points, At a Glance

- Take 30 minutes for yourself.
- Make yourself comfortable and relax.
- A lubricant is very helpful, but not absolutely necessary.
- Start with the nipples, the stomach, and the inner side of the thigh.
- Vary the manner of your touches.
- Stimulate the entire penis with various touches.
- Massage the scrotum.
- Explore the area between the anus and scrotum, and the anus itself, with circular motions.
- Switch back, as your level of arousal rises, to points you've already worked on.
- Use both hands – one for the penis and one for your expedition.
- Pay attention to the feelings that overcome you and that accompany the stimulation.

Pleasuring Yourself

In this chapter, we'll dedicate ourselves to love in its purest form: masturbation.

By the way, the Christian prohibition of masturbation rests on a misinterpretation of the Biblical story of Onan. The latter was punished because he hesitated to impregnate his brother's widow, as was the custom at the time. So this "sin" had nothing to do with masturbation. Even as a believing Christian, you can touch yourself with a clean conscience – you have my blessing in any case.

Masturbation is neither an alternative to sex, nor the other way around. Both fulfill the other, and masturbation can help to dissipate stored-up tension when one is more concerned with self-satisfaction than with intimacy. On the other hand, self-pleasure helps us to get to know our own bodies better, and to discover our sexual potential. Many women with orgasmic difficulties can overcome them once they've learned how to satisfy themselves. So, unbridle your pleasure, and have fun with your own body.

Maybe you've already had plenty of experience with masturbation. All the better! Then it'll come more easily for you to go through the exercises on this level, and the next. The solo exercises (kata) in the following belt level are a special kind of self-satisfaction – in some sense, with performance requirements.

If previously you've primarily masturbated with the help of pornography, then for the following exercise you should close the magazine and leave the movie on the shelf. In these exercises, the main thing is to concentrate on your own body. Scenes of couples in action can only distract you. You should rather direct your attention inwards, to get to know your own pleasure, instead of accepting someone else's understanding of pleasure. Only if you free yourself from your previous notions can you develop abilities that far exceed your previous power of imagination.

If you're attached to pornography, then later, as a blackbelt, I will give you a tip as to how you can have an especially great deal of fun with the MO-technique. But here, we're concerned with improving your abilities, and for this reason you should concentrate fully on yourself.

As has already been said: self-satisfaction is love in its purest form. Therefore, develop your love for your own body. Get to know it, accept its idiosyncrasies, and have fun with it.

But enough of theory already! What counts is practice. And satisfying yourself is something you learn best by satisfying yourself. Here are a couple more tips that will allow the practical implementation to become a special experience:

- Take the time you need for this kind of training.

- Ensure a surrounding that is free of distractions – so you can kick back without constantly worrying that you'll be discovered.

- Lie on a bed, or sit comfortably on a couch.

- With a lubricant or oil, you can make the experience even more intense.

- Vary your movements and discover new sources of pleasure that remained hidden from you as long as you were caught in the same old habits.

- Involve other erogenous zones in your self-pleasure. Use your "passive hand."

- Observe your body and its reactions. Follow your arousal curve.

4. The Green Belt

Green is the color of hope. Yeah, hopefully we'll finally get to the multiple orgasm, after all of this cuddling, you're thinking? Keep it slow – after all, you've only reached the green belt. But here, you'll take a big step further in the direction of your goal. We'll take a brief stroll through the mountains, and examine peaks, valleys, and plateaus. But since you're already familiar with my love of metaphors, you've already guessed that you won't have to leave your bedroom for this journey. Absolutely right, since here we have to do with the arousal curve, and for that, fresh mountain air is of less use to us than the calm ambiance of your bedroom.

Aroused - More Aroused - Erection

What is it with arousal? Are you aroused or not? And if so, how much? It's not easy to classify arousal, and a simple yes or no isn't enough for our goals. In this chapter, you'll learn how to distinguish the various levels of arousal.

At this point, I should perhaps clear up a misunderstanding right away: erection is not to be equated with arousal. True, the two often appear as a double-pack, but one can both be aroused without having an erection and have an erection without being aroused. In addition, many men get an erection with only slight arousal, while others only get one when arousal has advanced further. Independently of all that, the arousal level at which erection sets in also depends, for every man, on the shape he's in on any given day.

The goal of this belt level is to get to know the many facets of arousal, and to learn how to use them. By becoming more sensitive to the various degrees of arousal, you'll get to know your body more closely, and learn how to control it. For most men, arousal is a question of yes or no – or, at the most, with intermediary levels of "a little" and "a lot." As a multi-orgasmic man, you'll soon learn the ability to make much more varied pronouncements. Not that you'll often face the embarrassment of announcing your arousal level to others. But it will be an ability that will help you to better evaluate your own arousal.

Knowledge of the level of your own arousal and the techniques for influencing it are the key requirements for the MO-technique. You'll acquire the knowledge in this chapter, and the techniques in the following belt-exercises.

The Arousal Scale

But how can arousal be classified? For that, we'll introduce a simple 10-point scale. It reflects, from 1 to 10, the ten-point intervals in the percentage scale, from 1 to 100 percent. But how can one measure arousal? Well, for that, let's first take a look at the two extremes: 0 and 10.

Imagine that you've had a stressful work day, and are sitting in a traffic jam on the way home. You're thinking about how you can still manage to pick up some things at the supermarket and still be on time for the opening whistle of the big football match. You couldn't care less about sex at this moment, and there's no trace of arousal – nil, nada, niente. OK, that was a 0 – I think you get the picture.

Let's go to 10, which is just as easy to explain. 10 is orgasm – the big O, the finish line.

On the other hand, the intermediary levels are a bit more difficult to describe, since the 0 and 10 mark the only absolute values. The other levels can best be distinguished in relation to one another. In this way, you know that you've reached level 6 when you've clearly passed level 5, but have not yet reached the next level of arousal – level 7. To make the whole thing more visible, and to describe it in a less mathematical fashion, let's go through the steps one by one.

So, at level 1, you have a hint of arousal. Physically, nothing is noticeable yet, but there's at least an idea of sexuality in your head. At level 2, this idea takes shape, and your thoughts are sexual and erotic in nature. Your body shows its first reactions. Something's happening in your pants. Starting at level 3, the feeling in your pants is unmistakable. By now, your penis is bobbing like a divining rod that's struck a water source. You can still turn around and direct your attention at something else. Starting at level 4, your penis fills slowly with blood and swells, and your attention is more and more firmly set in the direction of sex.

At levels 5 and 6, arousal has you firmly in its grasp. The supreme commander in your pants has risen, and won't put up with any more resistance. At levels 7 and 8, your heart and breathing rates rise significantly. You're out of breath, like a jogger who's nearing the homestretch.

Level 9 is the homestretch. Here, everything is directed at the finish line – the orgasm. Your body is in the middle of ecstasy, and rushes towards the climax. You're probably already moist with sweat. Your surroundings sink into unimportance, and you find yourself, as Dorothy put it, "somewhere over the rainbow."

Just before level 10 – that is, near 9.9 – lies the "point of no return." Whether or not you know the term, you're certainly familiar with this feeling. At this point, it's clear that the orgasm is on its way. It's the turning point, or the breaking wave. It's that "yes, I'm coming!" feeling. I think you know what I mean.

This point is of decisive importance for the MO-technique. This is where the magic happens. But before you're capable of such powerful magic, we need to pay some attention to your wizard's staff.

Peaks, Valleys and Plateaus

Now we're getting to the exercise section. The picturesque title of this chapter has nothing to do with mountaintops, as we've already indicated. We're much more concerned with scaling the mountain of your arousal. In so doing, you can chart the ascent yourself, and set peaks in between. If for example you allow your arousal to rise to level 6, and then – by breaking off the stimulation – to drop again, then you've set a peak at level 6. If you then take up the stimulation again at level 4, then you've created a valley in your arousal curve. Valleys are of less interest for the MO-technique, but since they logically follow a peak, I mention them here for the sake of completeness. From this point on, we'll be concerning ourselves predominantly with the peaks.

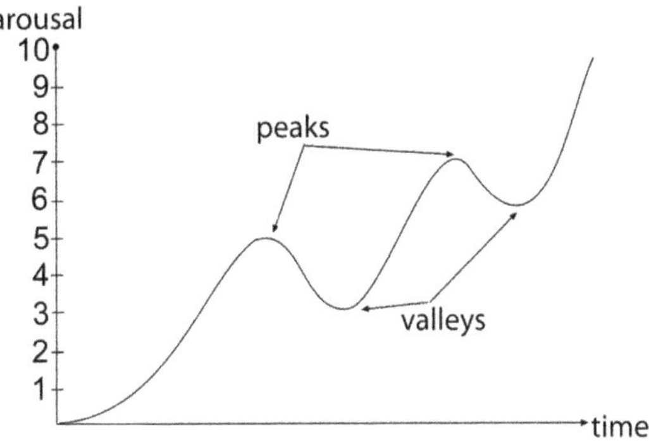

Illustration 6: Arousal Curve with peaks and valleys

I think you've grasped the concept. The plateaus are, correspondingly, peaks of a greater duration. You'll learn techniques for creating plateaus beginning with the purple belt. For the moment, we'll leave them aside, and look more closely at the peaks – and namely in practice.

Kata: Freeclimber

Before we begin with the exercise, I'd like to point out once more that the various levels of the arousal scale are purely subjective. At first, the practical application of this concept is perhaps something you're not used to. That's completely understandable, since previously you haven't divided your arousal into separate levels. For the MO-technique, this ability is of the greatest importance. You'll quickly learn to listen to the various signals your body gives, and to divide your arousal into different levels.

Since this is the first exercise that makes use of the arousal scale, take some time to experiment. Divide your scale in the way that makes sense to you. Soon you'll already be used to it, and correctly evaluate the level of your arousal. That alone is already a huge asset for your sexual abilities! And it will clear the way for you to learn the MO-technique.

Now let's get to the actual exercise. Once you've created comfortable surrounding conditions – see the chapter on "Exercise Preparation" – you can begin to stimulate yourself. In so doing, it's best to use the techniques that you learned during your voyage of discovery. Increase your arousal until you believe you've reached level 5. You can, for example, take the steady swelling of your member as an indicator for this level. Stop the stimulation, and breathe slowly and deeply, as you learned in the "Valley Wind" kata. Now this name takes on new meaning, since your peaceful breathing will calm your pulse and blow you gently from the peak in the direction of the valley. Make sure that all your muscles are fully relaxed. Observe how the swelling of your penis decreases, and how your arousal sinks. Wait until the arousal has fallen by at least two steps.

Congratulations! You've just created your first peak. As a reward, you may again raise the stimulation at level 3. This time, we'll go for a higher peak, at level 7. Go about it in the same way as described above. As soon as you've reached the peak, you should stop the arousal, breathe deeply, and relax your muscles. This time, let the arousal sink again by two levels – this time to level 5 – and then take up the stimulation once again.

After you've slowly developed a sense for the arousal scale, try now to press ahead to level 8. Then let yourself sink by two levels, and take up the arousal again. After you've finally established a peak at level 9, the exercise is over for today. If you want, you can go on to level 10 and relieve the pressure that may have built up.

You should carry out this kata several times, since you can learn a great deal about your arousal in this fashion. For each session, you shouldn't undertake any more than 4-5 peaks. Leave yourself enough time for the peaks (at least four minutes), and let the arousal rise slowly, over several peaks. Level 5 is a good start, but take care not to skip over more than two levels. Practice further, until you can set intermediary peaks (8.5 – 9.5). Here, just a few hand movements can set the level. With a little practice, you should be able to set peaks at 8, 8.5, 9, and 9.5 in a single session. If you manage that, then you're ready for the blue belt.

The Key Points, At a Glance

- Pay attention to your arousal during stimulation.
- Increase the arousal to level 5.
- Stop the stimulation and breathe deeply. Relax.
- Let the arousal sink by two levels, to level 3.
- Voilà – you've got a peak at level 5!
- Take up the stimulation again, and set a peak at level 7.
- Following every peak, let the arousal sink by two levels.
- Leave yourself at least four minutes for every peak.
- No more than 4-5 peaks per session.
- Practice until you can manage intermediary levels (8.5 – 9.5).
- The learning goal is reached with peaks at 8, 8.5, 9, and 9.5.
- Ending with ejaculation is OK, but not a must.

Kumite: Top Roping

Climbing in pairs with a rope safety is known as top roping. While one member of the pair climbs the wall, the other partner secures him from the ground. The comparison fits well, since, while you increase your arousal curve, your partner "secures" you. But have no fear! Any fall should end gently against the bed, on which you hopefully find yourself.

The two of you should begin your climbing session with a tender genital massage. While you lie relaxed on your back, your partner can pleasure you with her hands and mouth. If she notices that your arousal is rising, she should give you directions of something like the following: "Tell me when you're at level 5."

You should, in the meantime, concentrate on the rise of your arousal. Notice how you glide from one level to the next. When you believe you've reached level 5, then simply say only "five" or "now," or if you're a climber, you can also call out "stand" – although the latter may lead to confusion.

Your partner should then interrupt the stimulation. You yourself should then breathe deeply and take care to relax all your muscles. Observe how your arousal slowly abates. Once you've reached two levels lower – in this case, level 3 – you should give your partner a signal. This can be a thumbs-up or the OK-sign. Or you can just say "OK." The important thing is that the signs and signals be agreed upon beforehand, so that there are no communication difficulties during the exercise.

This was your first peak! Your partner begins to stimulate you anew – and this time, level 7 is the goal of your efforts. Once this is reached, say "seven," whereupon your partner will let go of you. Once again, your job is to breathe deeply, relax your muscles, and observe the drop in your arousal. And once again, you should allow the arousal to drop by two levels, in order to establish a clear peak at level 7. At 5, give your partner the agreed-upon sign again, whereupon she can begin stimulating again.

Repeat the above-listed steps and establish further peaks together at levels 8 and 9. In doing so, take enough time – that is, at least 3 minutes for every peak. It should be a pleasurable exercise, without any pressure. During the first attempt at this partner exercise, you can leave it at four peaks. But you should repeat the exercise without fail, in order to learn to set peaks at the intermediary levels of 8.5 and 9.5. Once you're in a position to set peaks at points 8, 8.5, 9, and 9.5 during a single session, then you've reached your learning goal, and can now proceed with the blue belt.

At the end of a session, in which you've set several high peaks, it may be the case that it's not possible for you, for a short time, to ejaculate the way you're used to. Have no fear. And this has nothing to do with the low oxygen levels at these high altitudes. You've simply overworked yourself for a brief period of time, which will end after approximately 10 minutes.

Out of fairness, you should ask your partner if she also enjoyed the climbing session. To ensure that, you can also carry out the exercise above, with the roles reversed. This has several advantages. First of all, she gets her efforts rewarded as well, and second, she too learns more about her own arousal. A further advantage is the fact that you learn more about her arousal curve as well. You will thereby learn to interpret the signs that she unconsciously transmits at various levels. This will have a lasting, positive impact on your sex, and you'll become a more experienced lover.

Whether you'd like to ejaculate at the end of the exercise or not is left up to you. You can also both go through the exercise, and close things off with some riotous sex. However your exercise takes shape – I wish you a lot of fun doing it!

The Key Points, At a Glance

- Begin with a gentle genital massage, during which your partner can pleasure you with her hands and mouth.
- Pay attention to your arousal during the stimulation.
- A direction, from her: "Tell me when you're at level 5."
- Let the arousal rise to level 5.
- Then say "five" or "now."
- She should break off the stimulation.
- You take a deep breath, relax your muscles, and observe the drop in your arousal.
- Let your arousal sink by two levels, to level 3.
- Voilà – a peak at level 5!
- Give her a sign, agreed upon beforehand, to take up the stimulation again (thumbs-up, an OK-sign).
- Take up the stimulation again and set a peak at level 7.
- After every peak, let your arousal sink by two levels.
- Allow at least 3 minutes for every peak.
- No more than 4-5 peaks per session.
- Practice until you can manage intermediary levels (8.5 – 9.5).
- The learning goal is reached with peaks at 8, 8.5, 9, and 9.5.
- Ending with ejaculation is OK, but isn't a must.
- Make an offer to your partner to carry out the exercise yourself, and pay attention to the signs she transmits as her arousal rises.

5. The Blue Belt

Greetings, mountain climber. I'm glad that you've learned to establish peaks, and have become more intimately acquainted with your arousal curve in the process. The arousal curve was an important step for the MO-technique, at least as important as a strong PC-muscle. While we're on the subject – are you also diligently performing your PC-muscle training? You should be, because you'll use it in this chapter. Yep, here it'll be put to use. You will learn, with its help, to stop not only your urine stream, but also your arousal…

The PC-Muscle as a Brake

Now that we've already dealt with karate and climbing, this time we'll do some bicycling. The PC-muscle can also be used as a brake. OK, that's it: the end of the metaphors. But don't rejoice just yet, because I'll come up with something for the next chapters, to inspire you with my metaphorical effusions.

But, back to the brake. A strong PC-muscle can bring your arousal under control. In the last chapter, you learned how to reach a peak by stopping stimulation. In this chapter, you'll learn how to establish a peak by flexing your PC-muscle. Basically, you can achieve this through the following techniques:

- Flex once, strongly and for a long time,
- flex twice, with medium strength, or
- flex briefly, several times in a row.

All of these methods work. It's best to try all of them, and find out which one works best for you. You'll get an opportunity to practice with the next exercises. As in the past, you again have the choice between solo and partner exercises – that is, between kata and kumite.

Kata: The Mountainbiker

Begin the exercise as you did the "Freeclimber" kata – with gentle stimulation. But when you reach level 5, don't stop there, but instead flex your PC-muscle – either once or twice, with considerable strength, or several times, briefly and intermittently. In addition, breathe in once, very slowly and deeply. Continue with the stimulation as you take your breath, and observe your arousal. Then relax all your muscles and interrupt your handwork. Allow your arousal to sink by two levels, before you start out on the path towards a higher peak.

You were surely able to detect, at this peak, how your arousal, despite further stimulation, remained constant. Perhaps you even experienced a slight drop in arousal. Nevertheless, for a drop of two levels, an interruption of stimulation is necessary.

Now try, in the same way, to establish peaks at 7, 8 and 9, and to maintain them. Notice that this technique becomes more difficult the higher your arousal rises. Therefore, at higher levels of arousal, you must flex your PC-muscle more strongly, and inhale longer and more deeply. It's the same as with a cyclist, who must press more strongly on the brakes in order to stop the bike at increasing speeds.

If, with the help of the PC-muscle and breathing, you can keep your arousal constant for a while, then the learning goal of this chapter has been reached, and you're ready for the purple belt.

The Key Points, At a Glance

- Pay attention to your arousal during stimulation.
- Increase the arousal to level 5.
- Flex your PC-muscle (once or twice for a long time, or several times briefly).
- Breathe in slowly and deeply. Observe your arousal.
- Interrupt the stimulation and relax your muscles.
- Let the arousal drop by two levels, to level 3.

- Set further peaks at levels 7, 8 and 9.

- The higher you go, the longer and more deeply you should breathe.

- The higher you go, the more strongly you should flex your PC-muscle.

Kumite: The Tandem

Begin the exercise in a comfortable atmosphere, with a gentle genital massage. Your partner can pleasure you with her hands or mouth. In so doing, she should go about things very slowly and tenderly, to give you the chance to feel the various levels of arousal. As a well-practiced climbing team, you already have experience with the various signals, which is why I won't go into that again.

Once you've reached level 5, flex your PC-muscle, either once or twice for a long time, or several times briefly. In addition, breathe slowly and deeply. You can also do this audibly, so that your partner knows when things have gotten that far. She should nevertheless gently maintain the stimulation to the very end of the breath, and only then stop – either on her own, or at your signal. Then, allow your arousal to drop by two levels.

Observe your arousal during this manoeuvre. It should, despite continuing stimulation, not rise any further. Use the subsequent interruption to completely relax and allow the arousal to drop again.

In the same way, establish peaks at levels 7, 8, and 9. The higher the level, the most strongly you'll have to flex the PC-muscle, and the long and more deeply you'll have to breathe.

The two of you should do this exercise several times with each other. When you've mastered it in the way described above, and have developed a sense of control through the use of your PC-muscle, you can also try the following variations. The advanced version of this exercise will be especially appealing to your partner.

Following the first peak at level 5, the two of you should assume a comfortable position. A variation of the missionary position is particularly well-suited, in which the woman props up her pelvis with a pillow, and the man kneels between her legs, without having to support himself with his hands. This is important, since the man should assume a position that is as relaxed as possible, without additionally tensing up any muscles. A further position that works well is when he lies on his back, and she sits on him. With this position, he can relax completely and concentrate unimpeded on his arousal. The “doggy-style” position works less well in this exercise. In this position, she kneels on all fours in front of him, while he enters her from behind. In this position, the vagina is especially narrow, which makes orgasm control more difficult for him.

Regardless of which position you decide on, begin with slow, deep strokes. Let your arousal slowly rise. At level 7, take an audibly deep breath, and simultaneously flex your PC-muscle. Following your breath, tell her: “That’s a 7.” Then she should stop her movements and wait until your arousal has sunk by 2 levels. Repeat these steps in order to establish peaks at levels 8 and 9.

Practice often enough to develop a sense of control using the PC-muscle. When you feel confident with it, then you’re ready for the purple belt.

The Key Points, At a Glance

- Begin with a gentle genital massage with the hands and mouth.
- Pay attention to your arousal during stimulation.
- Raise the arousal to level 5.
- Flex your PC-muscle (once or twice for a long time, or several times briefly).
- Breathe in slowly and deeply. Observe your arousal.
- After the breath, she should interrupt the stimulation.

- Relax your muscles and let your arousal sink by two levels, to level 3.
- Set further peaks at levels 7, 8, and 9.
- The higher you go, the longer and more deeply you should breathe.
- The higher you go, the more strongly you should flex your PC-muscle.

For The Advanced:

- Following level 5, have sexual intercourse with long, deep strokes.
- At level 7, breathe slowly and deeply, and flex the PC-muscle.
- After the breath, let her know: “That’s a 7.”
- She remains completely motionless, and you also relax your muscles.
- Allow your arousal to sink by 2 levels.
- Set further peaks at levels 8 and 9.
- Have a lot of fun doing it!

6. The Purple Belt

And once again, I have to congratulate you. The fact that you've reached this level shows that you can use your PC-muscle effectively to prolong peaks. As I've mentioned previously, peaks with a longer duration are also called plateaus. In this chapter, everything revolves around these plateaus. You've learned one variant for reaching them with the PC-muscle technique in the previous chapter. In this chapter, you'll get to know three more methods for maintaining your arousal at a steady level.

The following illustration visualizes the course of the arousal curve, with plateaus.

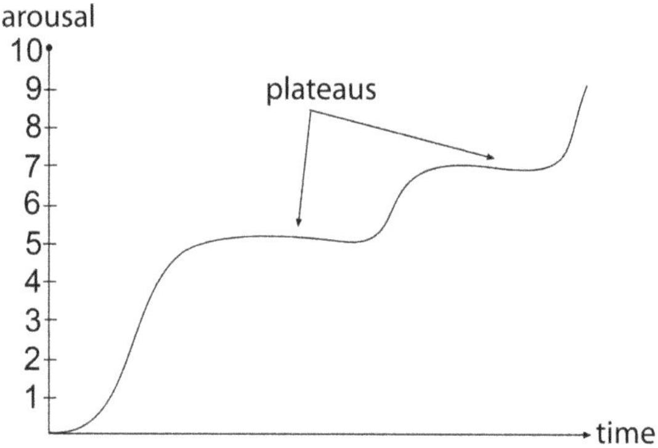

Illustration 7: Arousal Curve with Plateaus

The Art of Smoothing the Path

Now you know what plateaus are. With the PC-muscle, you've also managed to maintain small plateaus, of the length of a breath. Here, you'll learn of a couple of further methods for maintaining your arousal at a single level, and to do it for a longer period of time. Once you can hold your arousal constant over several minutes, then, sexually speaking, you're playing in the major leagues.

You have the following four tools at your disposal:

- The PC-muscle
- Breathing
- Variations of movement
- Shifting your attention

All variants work both singly and in combination. In the exercises, you'll first learn to train them in isolation. Finally, you'll combine them to attain the greatest possible control over your arousal curve.

Even if you're doing the partner exercises, you should read through the kata "Surfer," since the individual techniques are described there in detail. With the partner exercises, I only elaborate on the special characteristics of training with a partner.

Kata: The Surfer

As I've already threatened, now we have yet another metaphor. This time, we'll venture into the surf of the ocean. I'll show you how to ride out waves of varying heights. The size of the wave is to be compared to the level of your arousal. But before you can start surfing, you first have to paddle out.

To do so, start with a tender genital massage, as you've become familiar with in the previous chapters. Increase your arousal slowly and constantly until you've reached level 5.

As the first technique, we'll deal with breathing. Once you've reached level 5, slow down your breathing. You should continue with the stimulation, with the same long movements. Also, you should change nothing else, aside from your breathing. With this technique, it should be possible for you to slightly lower your arousal – by approximately half a level. Your sight should, in the meantime, have been trained to notice the finest facets of the arousal curve. If your arousal has dropped below level 5, accelerate your breathing to a rapid panting, until your arousal begins rising again. Attempt, with both breathing variations, to level off at 5, while you continue the stimulation in the same manner.

Hey dude, you're riding the wave! Yeah, now you've got it. Try to keep your surfboard in the middle portion of the wave. Vary the position by means of the corrective measures named above.

Don't experiment for too long with this technique, since it can lead, under rare conditions, to hyperventilation. 15 seconds are more than sufficient. Less is also OK. Enjoy the experience for as long as it lasts. Only the rarest waves last that long. The main thing is that you have a sense of how to actively ride out the wave.

A brief pause for relaxation. Allow yourself to move a bit in the direction of the shore, and then begin paddling out again – that is, stimulating – until you spot a size-6 wave. As soon as it's reached you, begin with the next method of wave-riding – by means of the PC-muscle.

Paddle further, until you're sure that the wave will take you along (6.5). Then flex your PC-muscle several times, strongly, without interrupting the stimulation. This should keep your arousal on a single level, and keep you on the wave. As soon as you notice that you're threatening to pass over the crest of the wave, flex your PC-muscle several times, once again. That will allow you to glide back down the wave and hold your position in the middle portion. Be satisfied here with a 15-second-long ride – if it even lasts that long.

If things have worked so far, then we can venture towards higher waves. Paddle out again and look for a size-7 wave. This time, you'll only vary the movement of your stimulating hand. That means that as soon as you've passed level 7, you should slow down the movements of your hand. With that, the arousal should decrease almost immediately. By accelerating the movement, you can once again increase the arousal. Experiment with this technique, until you can ride out this wave too for 15 seconds.

The last technique for riding out a wave is transferring concentration – in this case, shifting the pressure. If, on your board, you put your weight on your front foot, then you'll accelerate your motion. If you stand primarily on the back foot, your surfboard will move more slowly. In our case, that means that you can vary the pressure of your active hand in order to control your arousal. If you decrease the pressure, arousal will sink; if you increase the pressure, it will rise. Besides that, you can put the board in various positions – for example, completely forwards, on its nose. Here, the comparison with the penis really jumps out at you. Stimulate the penis at different places, with varying grip techniques. Try to ride out a size-8 wave for 15 seconds with this technique.

After you've learned how it goes, you should go surfing more often. Experiment with the different techniques, and, finally, dare to challenge size-9 and size-9.5 waves, until you can successfully ride them out. For waves of this size, you'll need all of your abilities – that is, you should combine the various techniques in order to surf waves of this size.

The Key Points, At a Glance

- Stimulate yourself with long, constant motions.
- Increase your arousal until you've passed level 5.
- Slow down your breathing only until you're once again below level 5.
- Accelerate your breathing, to allow your arousal to increase.
- Level off at 5, using both variants, and ride the wave for 10-15 seconds.
- Relax and let your arousal fall by two levels.
- Stimulate yourself with constant motion, up to level 6.
- Upon passing level 6, flex the PC-muscle several times, in order to maintain your arousal level.
- Keep up the movements, and attempt to ride the wave with the help of the PC-muscle.
- Relax, and let your arousal drop by two levels.
- Stimulate yourself with constant movements, up to level 7.

- Stick with the nature of the movement, but slow it down, until you fall below level 7.
- Accelerate the motion until you once again pass level 7.
- Ride the wave by varying the speed.
- Relax, and let your arousal drop by two levels.
- Stimulate yourself with constant movement up to level 8.
- Change the concentration of your movement – the pressure, or the spot at which you touch your penis.
- Vary things until you're able to ride level 8 in this way.
- With all techniques, remain relaxed, and concentrate on the level of your arousal.
- Combine the techniques in the later sessions, in order to ride size-9 and size-9.5 waves as well.

Kumite: Permanent Wave

You can also go surfing with your partner. In order to do so, the two of you should first read through the preceding "surfer" kata, since the individual techniques are explained there in detail. In describing the partner exercise, I'll limit myself to the particularities and variations.

You should begin with a tender genital massage. Your partner should pleasure you with long and even touches, so that you can fully concentrate on the various techniques. As she does so, you should lie, relaxed, on your back.

You can carry out the control by means of breathing and the PC-muscle, just as in the solo exercises. Ride the size-5 wave by varying the breathing, and the level 6 by contracting the PC-muscle.

In between waves, she should give you a break for relaxation, and let your arousal sink by two levels.

At level 7, with the variation of speed, it's important that you give your partner signals. That way, she'll know whether she should accelerate or decelerate the movement. Since you're lying relaxed on your back, you could, for example, keep your arm lying, relaxed, beside your body, and simply raise your thumb if she should accelerate the movements. When you pass beyond level 7, then lay your hand back flat on the bed, and she'll know that she should slow down the tempo. Try to ride the size-7 in this manner.

One special point comes up with shifting your concentration. While the surfer changes the location or the strength of the touching, we'll limit ourselves during the partner exercise to a mental shifting of concentration. During the "breath of wind" exercise on sensual touching, you learned to concentrate on the place where you're being touched. In this case, you must direct your attention to another place that is not being touched. For example, if your partner stimulates the penis, and you're crossing beyond level 8, then make a conscious effort to concentrate on another body part – for example, the scrotum, or your stomach – until your arousal drops. You can also concentrate on a body part of your partner. As soon as your arousal sinks back beneath level 8, direct your attention once again to the body part that is being touched. Try to ride the size-8 wave in this fashion. With this shifting of attention, you'll remain, in any case, spiritually on the ball, and won't take flight into unpleasant thoughts, such as, for example, Barbara Bush in a bikini, in order to force your arousal to drop.

Just as with the "tandem" partner exercise, you can, as an advanced learner, involve sexual intercourse as well. It is extremely stimulating for your partner if you ride out waves while you're inside her. It will be a great pleasure for both of you. The techniques also work as during genital massage, with the only difference being that you yourself have more control.

While controlling through varying the speed, you can, in this case, even determine the tempo yourself. And by shifting your concentration, you can, along with mental shifting, also vary your stroke technique. Thus, for example, you can alternate between shallow and deep strokes.

With increasing experience in the particular techniques, you can also begin to combine the methods. This will grant you access to larger waves (9 and 9.5), and longer wave rides. If your partner feels like it, she can also actively give this exercise a try herself.

The Key Points, At a Glance

- Begin with a genital massage, with long, constant movements.
- Increase the stimulation until you have crossed level 5.
- Slow down your breathing only, until you've dropped beneath it once again.
- Accelerate your breathing, to allow your stimulation to increase.
- Use both methods to level out at level 5, and ride the wave for 10 to 15 seconds.
- Continue stimulation until you reach level 6.
- When crossing level 6, flex the PC-muscle several times until the arousal drops.
- Keep up the movements, and attempt to ride the wave with the help of the PC-muscle.
- Continue stimulation until level 7.
- Your partner should stick with the manner of movement, but, at your signal, she should slow down its speed until you fall below level 7.
- At your signal, she should accelerate the movement until you once again cross level 7.
- Ride the wave by varying the speed.
- Continue stimulation until level 8.
- Shift your attention consciously to a body part that is not being stimulated, in order to lower your arousal.
- Concentrate once again on the spot of arousal once you've fallen below level 8.

- Vary until you're able to ride a size-8 in this fashion.

- With all techniques, remain relaxed, and concentrate on your level of arousal.

- During the waves, let your arousal sink by two levels.

- Combine the techniques in later sessions in order to ride size 9 and 9.5 waves as well.

For The Advanced:

- Sexual intercourse with slow, deep strokes.

- Variation of breathing and flexing of the PC-muscles in order to ride out the waves.

- Vary the speed in order to level out at a given level.

- Change the depth of your strokes, and mentally shift your concentration in order to maintain the level.

- Combine the techniques in later sessions, in order to ride size 9 and 9.5 waves as well.

7. The Brown Belt

If you've made your way through all of the exercises up to now, you've already come a long way. You've gotten to know the PC-muscle; hopefully, you've sufficiently trained it, and you can already control your arousal curve with its help. In the meantime, you know all about your individual arousal scale, and have become familiar with further techniques, beyond the PC-muscle, that you can use to influence it. In addition, you've been pretty active. You've been on a "voyage of discovery," climbed peaks as a "freeclimber" and a "mountain biker," and ridden out waves of arousal as a "surfer."

With the brown belt, you've now risen to the upper level of the belt system, and have learned the basic techniques needed to control your arousal. Now you're ready to learn the MO-technique. Up to now, in the exercises, we haven't ventured to confront the orgasm directly. From this point on, things will be different, because you'll learn how to experience not just one, but several orgasms.

As I already mentioned at the beginning of the book, in order for this to happen, it is necessary to separate the orgasm from the ejaculation. As a final preparation for multiple orgasms, ejaculation control is therefore the focal point of this chapter. I'll present various techniques, with the help of which you can suppress and delay ejaculation. You've already gotten to know some of them in the previous chapter, on controlling your arousal. Others are new, and will therefore be explained thoroughly.

In this chapter, I've done without a detailed description of solo and partner exercises. But that doesn't mean that you don't need to do any exercises for the brown belt. By now, you have enough experience to independently apply the individual techniques in practice, based on their description. For your first attempts at a particular method, I recommend that you practice alone. Once you've mastered a technique, then you can integrate it into sex with your partner as well. Have fun giving it a try!

Breathing

You've already become familiar with breathing as a means for controlling arousal, for maintaining a certain level of arousal, and for riding out a wave. But even at high levels of arousal (9.5 and higher), you can delay ejaculation with the help of breathing. An especially effective technique is to breathe in deeply just before ejaculation, and hold your breath until the urge to ejaculate subsides. For many men, this technique works the best.

For some multi-orgasmic men, on the other hand, breathing especially quickly and shallowly in order to delay ejaculation has proven effective. This breathing technique is also found in yoga, where it is known as "fire breathing." The Tao theory behind it is that one can use this breathing technique to distribute sexual energy throughout the body, where with long, deep breaths. it is easier to control the energy.

I advise you to work first with deep breaths, since you've already learned this technique during your wave-riding. It's very difficult to bring your ejaculation under control with breathing alone. But the breathing technique works especially well in combination with the PC-muscle, and should therefore be practiced without fail.

The Squeeze Technique

One more classical method for avoiding premature ejaculation is the so-called squeeze technique. It's found frequently in the relevant literature, and is one variant for causing arousal to sink.

The execution is relatively simple. Grab the penis just beneath the glans, with your index and middle finger on the underside of the shaft. Then, place your thumb on the upper side – opposite the two fingers – and squeeze firmly until the arousal subsides. Many men have more success with this technique if they use the same grip further down, near the base of the penis. The best thing is to experiment with this technique while pleasuring yourself, in order to find out what works best for you.

And here, we come right away to the disadvantage of this technique. While it can be used without problem during masturbation, it is more disruptive during sexual intercourse, since your member has to be pulled out of the vagina. Therefore, in practice, the other methods are to be preferred to the "squeeze technique."

If you have experience with visualization techniques, then you can carry out this technique mentally as well – that is, without physical pressure, and thereby support the other methods. Give it a try, but don't expend too much energy on this technique, because you'll soon get to know some that are more practical.

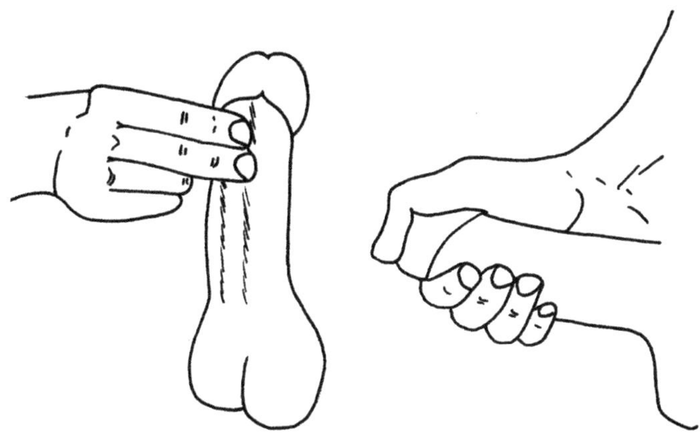

Illustration 8: The Squeeze Technique

The Testicle-Tug

Tugging your testicles? Ouch, that doesn't sound too pleasant. Have no fear, we aren't planning on pulling off your testes, but simply distancing them a bit from the body.

During ejaculation, the testicles are pulled up high and close to the body, so that the semen can be directed outward. It's fascinating to observe this process first-hand. By pulling the testes away, the expulsion of semen is postponed.

To do it, place your thumb and index finger, in the shape of a ring, around your scrotum, and carefully pull it away from the body.

"Let's have fun, said Farmer Bell, and shoved his ball-sack in as well." Unless your name is Farmer Bell, we can assume that your testicles are freely accessible during intercourse. Therefore, this technique also works as an auxiliary measure during sex.

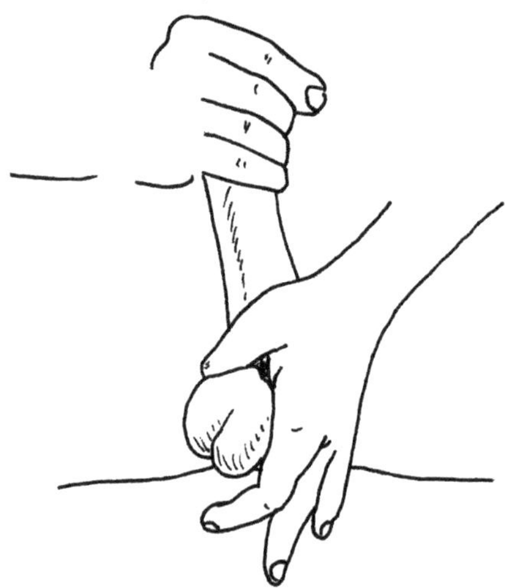

Illustration 9: Testicle-Tug

The Point of a Million Gold Coins

You've already become familiar with this point as an erogenous zone. Now, if you transfer the corresponding amount to my bank account, then I'll let you in on how one can put it to use in controlling ejaculation. What, you don't have a million? OK, taking into account the rate of inflation since the time of the Taoist discovery, we'll assume that the purchase price of this book will justify this revelation. Once again, you'll have gotten your money's worth, although this point is definitely worth it. Namely, with the proper technique, you can indeed use it to completely suppress ejaculation, while you have an orgasm. If done properly, your erection will remain afterwards, which makes multiple orgasms possible.

You've already learned where the point is situated. It's located on the perineum, between the anus and the scrotum, actually a bit closer to the anus. Use your three middle fingers to carefully feel out the small indentation.

When you cross the point of no return – that is, 9.9 on our scale – then press on this point with the three fingers, and simultaneously flex your PC-muscle. You must really press hard in order to suppress ejaculation. Breathe in deeply, wait for the contractions of the prostate to cease, and then continue stimulation. If you've done everything correctly, then your erection will remain. Perhaps its hardness will decrease slightly, but in any case, you'll be able to keep it up.

If your erection weakens, although no semen came out, then you probably had a retrograde ejaculation. Retro…what? It's an ejaculation that's directed inward, during which the semen is led through the urethra into the bladder. Whether or not this has in fact happened can be determined if you urinate into a glass and check to see whether traces of semen are found in your urine.

Have no fear, a retrograde ejaculation isn't harmful – it's just that it's not the goal of this exercise. Certain sects used this technique as a means of birth control. But I can't encourage that, since it can always so happen that an enterprising sperm cell makes its way to freedom.

If you feel an uncomfortable pressure or slight pain following this technique, then you probably pressed too late and too far forward. In order to avoid a possible feeling of pressure, you should massage your perineum with circular movements.

You can best practice this method by masturbating. When doing so, you can experiment with pressure, timing, and position. Once you've gotten a grip on the technique, give it a try during sex. But this method too is only an auxiliary means, in case your PC-muscle isn't sufficiently trained. The real king of the disciplines in terms of MO-technique is control by way of the PC-muscle.

Contractions of the PC-Muscle

Suppressing ejaculation with the help of the PC muscle is the real goal. At the moment of orgasm, you don't need to tug on your testicles, squeeze your penis, or press on your perineum. The PC-muscle alone can control the contractions of the prostate and the surrounding pelvic muscles. But a strong PC-muscle is indispensable for the successful use of this technique. Therefore, I've continuously urged you to carry out your training in a conscientious manner. If you've done this diligently up to this point, you'll now reap the fruits of what you've sown.

The technique is relatively simple, since you've already learned the foundations (arousal scale, breathing and PC-training). In the moment where you're crossing the point of no return (9.9), stop the stimulation, breathe deeply, and flex the PC-muscle as strongly as you can.

That was only the basic explanation of the technique. When you come to the black belt, you'll learn this method in more detail, and supported by exercises. I recommend that you try out the other techniques in this chapter on yourself initially, in order to learn them. Perhaps one of them will work especially well for you.

If your PC-muscle is strong enough, and you can hardly wait any more, then you may also proceed directly with the black belt. There, you'll learn the M.O. technique to perfection.

8. The Black Belt

Now you've made it to the black belt. In this chapter, you'll master the M.O. technique. That's the good news. The bad news is that this doesn't mark the end of your journey towards true mastery.

The first black belt (the first dan) only shows, in both karate and the MO-technique, that the student has mastered the technical basics. Or, as one says in karate, "karate-do begins where technique ends." But in fact this isn't bad news, because in the "master level" chapter, I'll show you how to get the most out of the MO-technique. That sounds promising, right?

Orgasm and Ejaculation

But then, you're not a blackbelt just yet, because first you have to separate the O from the E. What could I possibly mean by that? Orgasm and ejaculation, of course. Because, as you already know, that's the goal. We want to separate the two in order to suppress ejaculation, to experience orgasm in isolation. And not just one, but several.

For that, we still need to take a brief look at what happens during an ejaculation. As we have mentioned already, ejaculation is divided into: the contraction phase and the expulsion phase. During the contraction phase, the muscles around the prostate contract, and the semen is led into the urethra. During the expulsion phase, the semen is shot out by the rhythmic contractions of the PC-muscle. First the gun is cocked, and then fired. In the process, the contractions of the PC-muscle occur involuntarily, as a reflex.

All of this happens once the point of no return has been passed – that is, between levels 9.9 and 10. A time window is left of approximately two seconds. This is more than enough time. Since, during orgasm, we normally don't direct our attention to what's going on in our body, these proceedings usually remain concealed from us.

I therefore recommend to you as a preparation for the actual exercise to observe this phase in your own body, during a round of masturbation. To do so, you can pleasure yourself as usual.

On your way to the summit, establish a couple of peaks, and then steer resolutely towards the orgasm. When you're crossing the point of no return, stop the stimulation, relax, and concentrate fully on what's happening in your body. Can you feel how the semen is being gathered? How much time do you have until the contractions of the PC-muscle set in? Pay close attention to the feeling. Once you've done this exercise, you're ready for the final belt test of the MO-technique. Once again, it's up to you whether you practice alone or with a partner.

Kata: Implosion

You're certainly already very anxious and full of anticipation for your first multiple orgasm. OK, then I won't torture you any longer, and start right in with the exercise description.

Begin the exercise, as usual, with a genital massage, and a peak at level 5. Flex your PC-muscle and inhale deeply. Interrupt the stimulation, and relax, until the arousal falls off by two levels. Then begin the stimulation anew.

That was the warm-up round. Repeat the previous steps at levels 7, 8 and 9. Take sufficient time for every peak (at least 3 minutes).

And now things will get interesting. Observe your arousal attentively, in order to notice that you're headed towards the point of no return. In the moment when you're crossing it, flex the PC-muscle as hard as you can, and hold the tension for at least 10 seconds. Simultaneously, breathe in deeply, and hold the breath briefly, before calmly and deeply resuming breathing.

Can you feel the automatic contractions around the prostate? You're holding them in check with the PC-muscle. You can support this moment by a simple visualization technique. Imagine the PC-muscle as a fist closed around the prostate. You can imagine the prostate as a pulsating red ball. Now, squeeze the ball together firmly with your "PC-fist," until the ball stops twitching. This support will help you with your control.

The eyes are important as well. On this point, opinions diverge, in literature and in practice. The sexual researchers Riskin and Keesling firmly recommend that the eyes be left open, because the technique doesn't work otherwise. The Taoists Chia and Arava draw on the Taoist teaching that the various ring muscles (the eye, the anus, the mouth, and the PC-muscles) are linked together, and that a simultaneous shutting of the eyes and mouth support the contractions of the PC-muscle. I personally tend to keep my eyes open when I'm coming. But I also know men who have successfully applied the technique with their eyes tightly shut. It's best to give both a try, and make a conscious effort to pay attention to your eyes, particularly if it doesn't work straightaway.

Interrupt stimulation for as long as the PC-muscle remains tense. As soon as you detect that the contractions are diminishing, and that you have the situation under control, resume the stimulation slowly in order to maintain your erection. It may decrease in hardness for a short period,, but you should be able, to build it back up without any problem through further stimulation,.

Here comes the final spurt! Step on the gas one last time, and tear over the finish line – this time, with ejaculation. Don't hold anything back, but simply give yourself over completely to the second orgasm.

If everything's worked, then the second orgasm was your first multiple orgasm. Congratulations! If it didn't work on the first attempt, don't be discouraged, but keep trying until it works. Try to pay special attention to the interplay of timing, breathing, and PC-flexing, until you have success.

If it worked, it may be the case that the orgasms didn't feel "real." To explain this and other reactions, I offer a few tips in the chapter "1 + 1 < 2," following the partner exercise.

Now you're probably covered in sweat, and exhausted. Therefore, go take a shower before reading any further.

The Key Points, At a Glance

- Begin stimulation as usual, with a peak at level 5.
- Set the peak using the PC-muscle. Inhale deeply.
- Allow your arousal to sink by two levels, and then continue.
- Repeat the previous steps, with peaks at levels 7, 8 and 9. Leave at least 3 minutes for each peak.
- Venture towards level 9.9, with full attention.
- As soon as you're crossing the point of no return, flex the PC-muscle for 10 seconds, as hard as you can.
- While doing so, breathe in deeply and hold the air in briefly. Then, resume breathing, calmly and deeply.
- Pay attention to the contractions that you keep in check with your PC-muscle. Support the flexing through visualization.
- Pay attention to your eyes. First try the technique with open eyes. If it doesn't work, repeat with your eyes firmly shut.
- Interrupt stimulation for the duration of the flexing. Afterwards, continue with the stimulation, in order to maintain the erection.
- The final spurt: Go for the second orgasm. Give it your all! Don't hold anything back, and ejaculate.
- Give yourself a pat on the back, and hit the showers.

Kumite: Fusion

Now it's time for you and your partner to get busy with the final exercise for multiple orgasm. I have no desire to hold back your zeal with long introductions, so we'll get right down to business.

Begin, as always, with a gentle genital massage. By now that's probably become very familiar to you. You already know the further steps as well, so I'll only describe them briefly. With the help of the PC-muscle, set a peak at level 5, breathe in deeply, and allow your arousal to sink by two levels. Then, begin with sexual intercourse, and reach further peaks at 7, 8 and 9. Leave yourself enough time for each peak. In doing so, give your PC-muscle a good warm-up, because it's got a big task just ahead of it.

And now things get interesting. When you're headed for level 9.9, let your partner know about it. She can support you by lying completely still, in order not to make the technique difficult for you by too much friction. When you're spilling over the point of no return, there are several things that you must do at once.

Flex the PC-muscle as hard as you can, and hold the pressure for 10 seconds. Interrupt your movements, and breathe in as deeply as you can. Hold the air in briefly, then continue breathing calmly and deeply. Notice the automatic contractions that you're keeping in check with your flexed PC-muscle. You can support this aspect by imagining the PC-muscle as a fist that is closed shut around a round, pulsating ball. Squeeze firmly until the ball stops pulsating. It's better to keep the PC-muscle tensed up too long than too briefly, until the contractions let up.

Open your eyes! Many authors claim that this technique only works with open eyes. Other Taoist authors assume that one can support the PC-flexing by shutting the eyes and the mouth (on this point, see the kata "Implosion"). I advise you to leave your eyes open for the first attempt, and in the case of failure, you can experiment with your eyes firmly shut.

As soon as you notice that the contractions are letting up, and you're again master of the situation, you should continue with even thrusts in order to maintain the erection.

It may decrease a bit in hardness, but should be maintained through further stimulation.

Now launch into the final spurt, stepping firmly on the gas once more, and accelerating your arousal towards level 10. Dive into the orgasm without any tension, and with ejaculation.

Caress your partner and thank her for supporting you on your journey towards the multiple orgasm. This step has opened the door for you to many further sexual adventures that the two of you can hardly imagine at the present moment.

If it didn't work, don't worry. With a little practice, you too can make it happen. Experiment with timing, breathing, and PC-flexing, until you meet with success.

It may also be that you did have two orgasms, but both of them felt very unusual. Perhaps you also had unusual reactions that brought you little satisfaction. On this topic, read the following chapter, "1 + 1 < 2." It will answer a few questions for you, and do away with a few worries.

The Key Points, At a Glance

- Begin stimulation as usual, with a peak at level 5.
- Set the peak with the PC-muscle. Breathe in deeply.
- Allow your arousal to sink by two levels, and then continue.
- Begin with sexual intercourse, and set further peaks at levels 7, 8 and 9. Leave at least 3 minutes for each peak.
- Venture towards level 9.9 with full attention. Give your partner a sign, so that she can remain lying calmly from that point on.
- As soon as you're crossing the point of no return, flex the PC-muscle for 10 seconds, as hard as you can.
- While doing so, breathe in very deeply, and hold the air briefly. Then continue breathing, calmly and deeply.

- Pay attention to the contractions that you're keeping in check with your PC-muscle. Support the flexing with visualization.

- Pay attention to your eyes. First, try the technique with open eyes. If it doesn't work, repeat it with your eyes firmly shut.

- Interrupt your thrusts for the duration of the flex. Then, continue with slow thrusts in order to maintain your erection.

- The final spurt: Head for the second orgasm. Give it your all! Hold nothing back, and ejaculate.

- Hug and kiss your partner. Pamper her as a reward for accompanying you thus far on your journey.

1 + 1 < 2

There are very few men who experience two full and satisfying orgasms on the first attempt. The first time around, most men have the feeling that one orgasm slipped away from them, that it was only "half" felt, or that there was no orgasm with the concluding ejaculation. All these reactions are completely normal. Keep in mind that this was your first attempt. You were surely excited, and perhaps a little uptight. Besides, you were concentrating to the fullest, since you were taking a step into the unknown, and had to carry out several steps simultaneously. Of course, your body and mind must first get used to this new experience.

Maybe it was also very taxing and tiring, and you were therefore unable to enjoy your orgasm. You like it when you can simply give yourself over to the orgasm. I understand how you feel, but I can assure you that the first attempts cannot be compared with later practice, and your later experiences with multiple orgasms.

The first attempts might be compared to shooting a shotgun. You do everything you can to hit your target. The motto is: better too much than too little. You'll learn to fine-tune the entire process to such an extent that you'll require only the slightest possible effort. Then you'll become a sniper who hits his target with a single shot.

Then, a brief flex of the PC-muscle, at the right moment, is often all you'll need to experience a full orgasm – while keeping your erection.

As with any sort of learning, the MO-technique also proceeds consciously at first, and later unconsciously. It makes no difference whether you're learning to ride a bike, drive a car, or anything else – first you have to concentrate fully on all the steps. The more it becomes routine, the more the steps proceed automatically. At some point, you reach the stage where you can do other things while driving a car, because driving has entered your flesh and blood. It's much the same with the MO-technique as well.

And, as we've said: only now have you mastered the technique. From this point on, the master level begins. In the following chapters, you'll become familiar with various types of multi-orgasmic men. Further on, I'll show you a couple of advanced techniques, with which you can spread the orgasm throughout your entire body. There's a lot more to discover besides that.

There's a lot more awaiting you as well. Once you've mastered the technique of this chapter, you're ready for the secrets of the master.

6. The Master Level – For the Advanced

Hello blackbelt! What? You're not a blackbelt yet? Well then, turn back a few pages, because you should only tackle this chapter once you've mastered the technique. Well, OK, if you're already here, then you can peek ahead a bit.

If you've already come to grips with the technique, then here you can expect to find a thing or two to further refine your skills. You'll become familiar with various "battle styles," according to which you can apply the MO-technique. In addition, you'll get to know the higher dan levels in theory and in practice, which will help you to fully develop your sexual potential.

Now you're surely very excited already to learn what awaits you here. But before we come to the actual essence of this chapter, I must caution you once again…

Practice Makes Perfect

It's an inconvenient truth, I know, but it also applies to the black-belt. Especially if you master the technique to such a degree that you can pull off two orgasms, but find that this isn't enough for you. If you've made it this far, then you'll certainly manage to perfect the technique as well.

The important thing is that you continue to train your PC-muscle. If it's already strong enough to have managed the black belt exercise without any problem, then maintenance exercises will be sufficient. If you're still not confident regarding your PC-power, then you should continue with your buildup exercises, until you reach that point. As a maintenance exercise, I recommend that you continue to piss in spurts every time you visit the restroom. And a couple of "PC-jabs" and "PC-kicks" now and then will give you a strong PC-muscle for as long as you live, that, aside from sexuality, will also positively affect your health.

Don't be shy about returning to exercises from the lower belt ranks, in order to train particular weak spots in a targeted fashion. You yourself will best be able to value which of the necessary abilities you've now mastered with confidence, and which could still stand to be improved through targeted training. Just be glad that it's a stimulating hobby we're dealing with here, and that while the training may demand its share of sweat, it's no less enjoyable for all that.

The exercises I present here should allow you to fine-tune your abilities – once again, with or without a partner, as you choose. Meanwhile, I'll do without detailed descriptions of every particular step, while, at the same time, giving special emphasis to the goal of the training. Anyway, you're a blackbelt now, and you should know by now how, for example, to establish peaks and make use of your breathing.

Kumite: Dance Atop the Volcano

Begin, as always, with a peak at level 5, during a genital massage. As soon as your member is erect, enter your partner and establish a further peak at level 7 or 8. In setting your peak, use only your PC-muscle and breathing.

Now comes the demanding part of the exercise – the dance atop the volcano. The goal of the exercise is to reach several ascending peaks between levels 9 and 10, which you'll carry out with the help of PC-contractions of medium strength. That is, at levels 9.1, 9.2, 9.3… all the way to 9.9. You don't have to have ten of them, but each one should be a bit higher than the one before. If you can pull off ten peaks, then all the better. Note that when it comes to peaks at this altitude, the air is extremely thin. That is to say that the interval between a 9.1 and a 9.2 may consist of 1-3 thrusts. Pay conscious attention to how many thrusts lie between the particular levels. And try each time to go a bit further in order to create a new intermediary step. This part of the exercise will be extremely arousing for your partner, because you'll find yourself literally in a highly explosive situation.

Make your way peak by peak towards the point of no return, and be sure not to "spill over." As soon as you notice that things have come that far, give your partner a short signal for her to remain completely still for a moment. Flex your PC-muscle very firmly, and withstand the contractions. When they level out, continue your strokes, in order to maintain your erection. Allow your arousal to sink somewhat, and relax your muscles. As soon as you notice that your arousal is once again headed upwards, attempt yet another dry orgasm by repeating the above steps. If, however, you're already completely exhausted by ascending this peak, then you can also ejaculate now, and give yourself over to the final orgasm.

Every time you go through the exercise, shorten it by one peak during the peak-phase, and tack on another orgasm during the MO-phase. That way, you'll learn to bring the PC-muscle into play later and later, until you'll only need a single PC-squeeze to get past the first of several orgasms. Your partner will also get to know your rhythm better and better, and keep still at the right moment. The two of you will also be more attuned to each other, and dance atop the volcano together.

The Key Points, At a Glance

- Start out with a peak at level 5, and then, during intercourse, with another one at 7.
- Then establish as many peaks at as many intermediary levels as you can, from 9.1. to 9.9.
- Use medium-strength PC-muscle flexes at the peaks.
- Pay attention to the fine levels of arousal, which often consist of only a couple of strokes.
- As soon as you're crossing the point of no return, give your partner a signal, at which she should remain lying still.
- Flex your PC-muscle very firmly, inhale deeply and wait until your contractions let up. Enjoy the orgasm.
- Continue stimulation in order to maintain the erection.
- Attempt a second dry orgasm.
- Ejaculate the final time, if you feel like it.
- Embrace your partner and thank her for the dance atop the volcano.
- Ask her to dance at the next opportunity, and try each time to experience one less peak and one more orgasm.

Kata: Storming the Summit

This exercise works great as a solo-exercise, since it leaves you with complete control over your stimulation. Begin with a gentle peak at level 5, and with a further peak at 7 or 8. For this peak, and the following ones, apply medium PC-pressure, and pay attention to your breathing.

Now we're headed for the peak of the iceberg, and you'll try to pull off several ascending peaks between levels 9.1 and 9.9. Pay attention to the subtle differences between the particular levels, which often consist of only a couple of nuances of your thrust. If you carry out the strokes with your active hand, take note of how many strokes you need to climb a bit higher in terms of arousal.

Work your way, in this fashion, bit by bit, towards the point of no return. As soon as you notice that you've passed it, flex the PC muscle as firmly as you can, breath deeply, and, thus, retain control over your contractions. Enjoy the orgasm and pay conscious attention to the prickling sensation that envelops your body while you flex the PC-muscle in order to hold back the ejaculation.

As soon as you notice that the contractions are stopping, relax, and proceed carefully with the stimulation, in order to maintain your erection. Allow your arousal to subside a bit, or keep it at a high level, if that's more comfortable for you. Attempt a second dry orgasm by repeating the above steps. If you're already exhausted from the excitement of the previous peaks, you can also slide into the valley with your ejaculation-sleigh.

Such high-altitude training is good practice, so you should repeat it. With every repetition, do without one more peak during the approach, and tack on another orgasm at the end. In that way, you'll develop an ever greater feel for the right timing and the right pressure. For today, you've already accomplished enough, and earned yourself a shower.

The Key Points, At a Glance

- Begin stimulation, as usual, with a peak at level 5, and with a further one at 7 or 8.

- Add to that as many intermediary peaks as you can, from 9.1 to 9.9.

- At the peaks, use medium-strength PC-muscle pressure.

- Pay attention to the subtle degrees of arousal, often consisting of only a couple of thrusts.

- As soon as you cross the point of no return, flex the PC-muscle firmly, breathe deeply, and wait until the contractions let up. Enjoy the orgasm.

- Continue with the stimulation in order to maintain your erection.

- Attempt a second dry orgasm.

- Ejaculate the final time around, if you feel like it.

- Repeat the exercise, experiencing, each time around, one less peak, and one more orgasm.

Kata: Fireworks

Do you like pornography? Then this exercise is just right for you. While in the previous chapters you were cautioned against having your attention distracted by media stimulation, directing it instead towards your inner arousal, in this exercise you're explicitly allowed to make use of it. Pornography is effectively your exercise material – so fetch your magazines or videos from your secret stash, and whip out those knockers.

As you've notice by now, a masculine wind is blowing in this chapter; and for that, I'd like to apologize to my outraged female readers. You'd do best to skip this chapter, because in this exercise, you'll appear only as superficial, media-drive objects of lust.

If you're used to satisfying yourself using pornography, then this exercise will be especially fun for you. You surely know your collection well by now, and have a few favorites. Depending on where your preferences lie, you've surely selected pictures or film scenes for your climaxes that are perfectly suited for them. This fact makes a particularly stimulating training method possible.

It's not at all necessary to explain the separate steps. Stick to the directions from "Storming the Peak" in order to attain multiple orgasms. As motivation, use one of your favorites for each of these climaxes. Take, for example, one of your favorite pictures, or key the movie to your favorite scene, and try, during orgasm, to hold back the ejaculation with strong flexing of the PC-muscle. While doing so, take a deep breath. Hold the pressure until the contractions give way, and then continue the stimulation in order to maintain your erection. Now it's time to turn a few pages or fast-forward – to your next favorite piece of orgasm art.

The motivation that arises from this method makes the MO-technique interesting for self-pleasure above and beyond your training. This was just an example. Be creative, and make the training fit your individual preferences in order to extract the maximum benefit for yourself.

MO Fighting Styles

In Karate, as well as in Kung Fu, there are different fighting styles. Surely you've already heard something about the crane style, the eagle talon, or the tiger claw. There are different styles in the MO-technique as well. This means, that once you've learned it, the MO-technique can be applied in different ways. You can adopt the ability to have multiple orgasms to the situation at hand, and apply the different styles in different ways. Most men do, at some point, find the right MO-style for them.

The styles presented here are only examples, but they depict the majority of the different MO-types. There's no best technique; they're just different forms of the same ability.

Multi-Style

This style is what one thinks of the first time one hears of male multiple orgasm. Those who practice this variant normally take at least 10 minutes before they have their first orgasm without ejaculation. The sex can be continued without any big interruption, and, if you so desire, 2-5 more orgasms can be tacked on, each of approximately the same intensity. The final orgasm is accompanied by ejaculation. The advantage lies in the fact that you have a choice: longer or shorter – the multi-style allows you to adapt to any given situation.

Duo-Style

This style is especially for those men who had problems with premature ejaculation, before this program. The duo-style aims to achieve one orgasm for the man, and one for both partners. Men who prefer this style come the first time with a powerful, dry orgasm, after a relatively brief time period. After that it is much easier to last longer the second time. Using the PC-control they've learned, they can control their arousal very well, and ration out their arousal so that their second orgasm will coincide with that of their partner. Here, it's often helpful if the woman continues to lie still during the first orgasm (agree on a signal), to make the first orgasm easier on the man. This style is very well-suited for everyday sex. The goal is not to set performance records, but simply to have sex that is satisfying for both patners.

Shot-Style

Many men have multiple orgasms with ejaculations. That means that after the first orgasm with ejaculation, the level of arousal and the erection give way slightly. After a short pause – and without completely losing the erection – stimulation can be continued. During the second orgasm as well, the climax is accompanied by ejaculation. In this way, many men achieve up to 6 orgasms with ejaculation. Through their training, they have shortened their refraction phase to an extreme degree. This technique is advanced, and can't be learned by everyone.

Drop-Style

With this style, orgasm is, after 10-15 minutes, accompanied by a partial ejaculation. This first, very intense climax is then followed – through further, powerful strokes – by further, weaker orgasms, like aftershocks. This variant is an orgasm-model that is seen in many women.

Tao-Master-Style

The Tao-master makes do without ejaculation altogether! He experiences several full orgasms – much as with the multi-style – while doing without the closing ejaculation! He applies further techniques in order to increase the intensity of his orgasms, and to expand them throughout his entire body. The Tao-master ejaculates once a month. For the remaining orgasms, he retains his sexual energy within himself, lets it circulate within his body, and can even convert it and use it for other ends. Since he's gone without the ejaculating orgasm, he experiences no drop in energy after sex, like most men do. The typical experience of tiredness and exhaustion stay away. The Tao-master is energetically overloaded after sex, since he uses sex to raise his energy level. This is beneficial for his health as well.

This style represents something really special. Therefore, we'll occupy ourselves in greater detail with this technique, and with a couple more Taoist secrets.

Do Without Ejaculation?

Yes, you heard that right. Up until now, you've gotten to know the MO-technique as a possibility for experiencing several dry orgasms, before a final ejaculation. This practice reflects sex in our Western cultural context. But according to Taoist teachings, every ejaculation is also a loss of energy. Every man who's tired and exhausted after sex knows this loss of energy. No man can imagine carrying out great sporting feats right after sex.

But if one goes without ejaculation during the final orgasm as well, the energy remains in your body, and one feels fit and energetic after sex. True, you don't get that typical feeling of relief, but then, you don't feel tired either. Here, everyone should make the choice himself, based on the given situation, as to whether sexual congestion should be relieved, or whether sex should be used as an energy generator.

According to Taoist teachings, avoiding a loss of energy has positive effects for one's entire state of health. An organism with a high energy level is less susceptible to illnesses. Here, the Taoist view differs from other sexual-religious practices, in which ejaculation is avoided because the semen is considered holy.

It's up to everyone to decide for themselves where they stand with regard to all this. For some, it's all some esoteric hoax, but for others, it's worth a try, in order to learn something new. But it's also good to know what you're missing. Therefore, I'd encourage you to try out the following exercises for the Dan level. I can confirm, based on my own experience, that it's an exhilarating feeling to feel the sexual energy in the body, and to spread the orgasm throughout the entire body.

The Dan Levels – Shades of Black

There are increments in the master levels as well, although they're no longer designated by colors, as the student levels were. The exercises in this chapter deal with sexual energy. You'll become familiar with the minor and major energy cycles, as well as methods for controlling energy.

Beyond that, this chapter also deals with the satisfaction of your partner. I'll explain a couple of positions and thrust techniques to you, with which you can send your partner into ecstasy.

2. Dan – Energy

There is bioelectrical energy in every cell of our body. An exchange of energy also takes place inside the body. The most well-known here is the concept of Chi, from traditional Chinese medicine (TCM). Acupuncture has become more and more well-known in our cultur as well, and orthodox medicine is making ever more frequent use of this knowledge, won over the course of many centuries.

According to this teaching, the human body contains, along with the circulatory system and the lymphatic system, yet another energetic network: the meridians. These energy channels run thickly beneath the body's surface, and can best be influenced at certain points.

For our purposes, such a sophisticated system is far too detailed. Since we're not interested in healing certain illnesses or the interaction between the organs, a less refined understanding of the energy system is sufficient for us.

Just imagine to yourself that we're moving along the highway, and all of the small side streets don't interest us here. One of these highways is the small energy cycle.

The Minor Energy Cycle

The minor energy cycle is the highway upon which our sexual energy goes into motion. At this point, we'll first examine the map, before, in the next chapter, getting in the car and taking a ride.

According to Taoist thought, this cycle holds the key to the circulation of energy, and thus to an expansion of sexual pleasure.

But how does it feel when the energy in our body is flowing? The energy streams through our body on a permanent basis. But most of the time, we're not aware of it at all. That's because the concept of energy is less known in our cultural circle, and we therefore don't pay attention to it. People who deal for the first time with the conscious manipulation of this energy – for example, during acupuncture – often describe this as thrilling, electrifying, pulsating, tickling, or warming.

Most men can't trace the energy along the entire cycle. But they do sense the energy at certain points along this path. Therefore, it's important to know first off where this path is located. The minor energy cycle can be subdivided into a front and back channel.

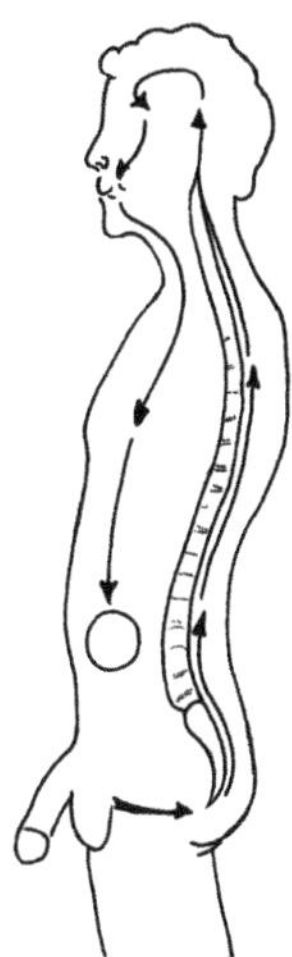

Illustration 10: Minor Energy Circle

The Back Channel

The back channel extends from the perineum across the back side of the body (the tailbone, vertebrae, and neck), reaching above to the crown of the head and back down to the brow. It ends just beneath the nose and above the upper lip.

The Front Channel

The front channel begins at the tip of the tongue and runs across the throat down the middle of the body's front side, down to the perineum. In pregnant women, the front channel sometimes shows itself as the so-called Linea Negra.

The two channels can be linked by pressing the tip of the tongue against the gums, in order to close the cycle. In so doing, the tongue works as a switch that starts the energy flowing.

Sexual Energy

Sexual energy is a very powerful form of the body's natural energy. As men, we feel it very clearly when we're overcome with horniness, and become sexually aroused. With the scale of arousal, in the student levels, you developed a kind of measuring device for this kind of energy, and were able to observe and steer the intensity of the rising energy.

But as masters of the MO-technique, we're not satisfied anymore with controlling the intensity; rather, we want to move this energy in our body in a targeted fashion.

3. Dan – Control of Sexual Energy

The control of sexual energy will come especially easy for you if you already have experience with meditation or other techniques of self-experience. But even if you have no previous knowledge, you'll soon learn to steer the energy in your body.

The goal is to pull the sexual energy from the genitals and distribute it within the body. And here, the highway of the minor energy cycle comes in quite handy. So, the energy is pulled out of the penis, across the perineum and the vertebrae. The first stopping point is then the head. If you manage to pull the energy up into the head, then you've already mastered the most difficult part.

But how does one move the energy inside the body? Energy follows concentration. It has been scientifically proven that one can increase the activity of nerves and muscles through targeted attention alone. We make use of this fact during the following exercises by consciously visualizing the energy's path. It may be that you can only feel the activity at certain points along this stretch. That's fully in order. It's just important to make yourself aware of the energy flow, in order to trace its movement.

I'll introduce an appropriate exercise for this in just a moment. But first, the hint must be given that it's hard to allow the energy to flow through the body if the back is kept tense. Tenseness forms blockades, and should therefore be dissipated before the exercises. So now would be the right time for a partner-massage or a bit of yoga.

Kata: Mountain Stream

In this exercise, you'll learn to control light sexual excitement and to transform it into vitalizing energy. This technique works especially well if you become aroused in some everyday situation, but have no possibility to release the tension. Besides that, it's much more efficient to actually use the energy than, for example, quite literally flushing it down the toilet. So, when that colleague of yours at work is wearing a short mini-skirt, or the next time a fashion model steps into the sauna, you'll know what to do.

The exercise is relatively simple, since the excitement is controlled when it arises. We now find ourselves at the source of the mountain stream, which hasn't yet become a thundering stream. As for how you can control "churned up" sexual energy – you'll learn that in the kata "Waterfall."

Begin the exercise by bringing your arousal to level 2. You can do this by thinking erotic thoughts or through light genital stimulation. As soon as you notice that the sexual energy is stirring, inhale deeply and hoist up your testicles a bit with a slight flex of your PC-muscle.

Exhale again, relax, and pay further attention to the rising sexual energy. Imagine that you're pulling the energy above the testicles into the tailbone. In so doing, you can visualize the energy as a silvery and glistening, or red and pulsating, mass, which is distributed slowly along the path which you determine. This was just an example. You can imagine the energy in whatever way you want, but it should be a picture that reflects the warm, prickling nature of the energy.

Alternate between inhaling and pulling and exhaling and relaxing. As soon as you notice that the sexual energy has spread and gathered back in the tailbone, you can let it rise up along the vertebrae. While doing so, you can imagine the backbone as a pipe through which you pull the energy upwards. As soon as you have gathered enough energy around the tailbone, you can support the PC-flexing by contracting the muscles of your rear end. With these, you can pump the energy up the vertebrae.

Experiment to see whether it's easier for you to pull the energy up or to pump it up. With increasing experience, it will become easier and easier for you to move the sexual energy. Often, all it takes is a short flex of the butt-muscles to drive the energy up the vertebrae.

As soon as the energy approaches your neck, draw your chin slightly backwards and straighten the back side of your neck, in order to free the way. Continue until you can sense the energy in your head. Use the hollow of your head as a place to gather the energy. I didn't mean to offend you just now – only to offer you a new image for your visualization technique.

When you've gathered enough energy in your head, try to let it circulate in your head. First in one direction, then in the other. That may sound strange now, but as soon as you've had the experience once, you'll understand what I mean.

It's not good to let the energy dwell in your head for an extended period. As the final disposal point, the stomach area behind the navel is best. In order to get the energy there, you must first press the tip of your tongue a bit against the gums behind your teeth. This allows the energy to flow to the front channel. You can support the downflow by swallowing your saliva.

Imagine how you load up the saliva with energy before you swallow it down. Let the energy flow down into your throat, over the solar plexus and into your abdomen. Here too, you can imagine the body once again as a hollow space, in which the energy flows from above.

The movement through the front channel is a bit harder, particularly for men. According to Taoist thought, the emotions dwell in this region. Since many men don't let their emotions out freely, but "bottle them up inside," or "swallow" their anger, these blockades are much like the tensing of the back muscles with the back channel. But with a little practice, you should succeed in overcoming these blockades. You can support the flow of energy by stroking with both your palms from the base of your throat down broadly across your chest. At the end of the stroking motion, your hands should rest on your stomach.

If you imagine the body as an electrical system, then the erotic spark first strikes at the base of the penis. The electricity that arises as a result (arousal) is then either shot out through the circuit breaker (ejaculation) or led by a lightning rod along the energy cycle. There, it serves to charge the inner battery in the abdomen, after it has flooded through the entire system and activated it. This comparison shows quite nicely how ejaculation, as well as the alternative, affects the balance of energy in your system.

The Key Points, At a Glance

- Make your way to arousal level 2, with erotic thoughts or light stimulation.

- As soon as your excitement stirs, inhale, and hoist your testicles a bit with a light flex of the PC-muscle.

- Visualize the energy – how it builds up and spreads.

- Pull the energy across the testicles into the tailbone.

- Alternate between inhaling and pulling and exhaling and relaxing.

- As soon as enough energy has gathered in the tailbone, use contractions of the butt-muscles to pump it up the spine.

- Pull your chin back a bit and stretch the back of your neck in order to pull the energy into your head.

- Allow the energy to circulate in your head. Note the prickling sensation.

- Press the tip of your tongue against your gums to draw down the energy.

- By swallowing, support the flow of energy down into the throat.

- Pull down the energy across the solar plexus into its final repository behind the navel.

- If you encounter blockades, support the downflow of energy by stroking with the hands.

4. Dan – Full-Body Orgasms

After you've learned to control less powerful currents, we'll head into the rapids of the mountain stream. As soon as the arousal increases, the river will become more and more raging. It's as if you were approaching a waterfall on a kayak. Therefore, you should master the "Mountain Stream" kata before you venture into the rapids and the "waterfall."

But once you've mastered the controlled ride through the rapids, then kayaking will become a full-body experience, and, by the same token, your orgasms will become full-body orgasms.

The Taoist theory behind the next exercise holds that an outpouring of semen can only take place if the nerves receive enough energy, and the muscles sufficient blood, in order to unleash the muscle spasm. The logical conclusion of this is to pull the blood from the genitals, and the energy from the genital nerves. This can be accomplished by flexing an important muscle group – first and foremost, the PC-muscle, of course. Its contractions are supported by the large buttock muscles, and, when necessary, by tensing the foot, fist, and jaw muscles. View this assistance by other muscles as training wheels that you'll no longer need once you've mastered the PC-bicycle. The stronger you train your PC-muscle to be, the more control it will be able to assume.

Kata: Whitewater Rapids

This is a very effective method for making use of aroused sexual energy. So, train - but not in bed. As soon as you've mastered the technique, you can, of course, apply it in bed as well.

Pleasure yourself until you've reached arousal level 6, and establish a short peak with the help of the PC-muscle. If you're just learning the technique, you should first practice alone. Later, you'll also be able to let the energy circulate in any situation you feel like. Don't practice just after eating, since energy is required for digestion, and, thus, the flow of energy becomes harder to observe. Besides, you should be well-balanced, since this exercise strengthens the emotions. So, if you're feeling angry, aggressive, or fearful, put off the exercise until you're back in harmony with yourself.

You should practice while standing or sitting. Continue with your self-pleasure until you're at level 8, and have a strong erection. At the next peak, at level 8.5, flex the PC-muscle powerfully. Simultaneously pull your butt-cheeks together until the energy has connected in your tailbone. Inhale deeply when you're moving the energy. To support the extraction out of the genitals, you can stomp on the floor with your toes, or clench your fists.

Then, you pump the energy up the spine with powerful butt-muscle contractions. In so doing, try to flex the entire buttock muscles, from your anus to your spinal column, in wavelike motions, in order to support the flow of energy. You can also rock your pelvis back and forth, like when riding a horse.

Pull the chin back and stretch your neck as soon as the energy has reached the neck vertebrae. Concentrate on the top of your skull, and use it as a magnet to pull the energy into the head. Additionally, you can look upwards with your eyes.

When the energy has made it to your head, the erection should have let up a bit. Now continue pleasuring yourself, in order to repeat the exercise anew at level 8.5. Continue the repetitions until enough energy has been gathered in your head. Then let it circulate a bit in your head, and enjoy the warmth and prickling sensation that spreads across your entire body. In the meantime, relax your muscles.

Stimulation is like driving a dynamo, with which you generate energy. Then you pull the energy through the system of cables up into the light bulb (the head), which immediately begins to shine. The more energy you generate and divert, the brighter the lamp will shine. And when you really step on the gas, then you'll have a genuine disco lightshow.

Here, also make sure to divert the sexual energy further, out of the head, so that the fuses don't blow. To that end, activate your tongue-switch, and let the energy flow down along the front side of your body, so that it can be stored in the stomach.

The Key Points, At a Glance

- Practice while standing or sitting, when you're emotionally balanced and have an empty stomach.

- Stimulate yourself and establish a peak at level 6, and a further peak at 8.5, with the PC-muscle. When doing so, flex the PC-muscle, the butt-muscles, and, perhaps, other muscles (hands, feet) firmly, in order to pull the energy out of the genitals, across the perineum and into the tailbone. Inhale deeply while doing so.

- If a bit of energy has gathered in the tailbone, then pump it, with wavelike movements of the pelvic muscles, up the spine. Then inhale, using short breaths.

- Visualize how the energy is spreading.

- Pull back your chin slightly and stretch your neck, in order to pull the energy into your head. Look upwards, and magnetically attract the energy with the top of your skull.

- Observe how the erection lets up, and continue with stimulation, in order to generate even more energy, which you then gather in your head.

- Repeat these steps 3-6 times, until enough energy has been gathered.

- Let the energy circulate in your head. Feel the prickling sensation. Relax the muscles.

- Press the tip of your tongue against the gums, in order to pull down the energy. Draw the energy down across the solar plexus into the final collection place behind the navel.

Kata: Waterfall

This exercise is a combination of the "Whitewater Rapids" and the "Storming the Summit" katas. It has to do not only with blocking off the energy during multiple orgasms, but with diverting it. The diverted energy then serves not only the local contractions in the genital area, but is pulled into the entire body, in order to spread the orgasm.

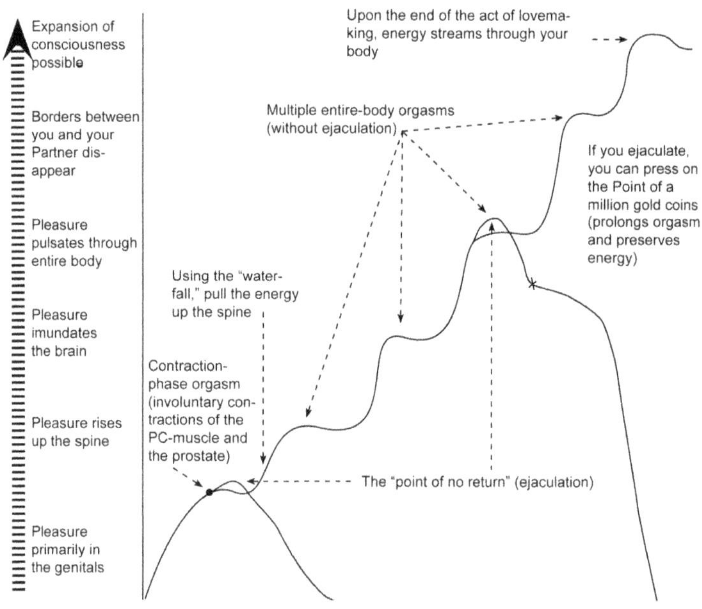

Illustration 11: Orgasm Potential (Source: Chia/ Abrams Arava

The basic prerequisite in order to fully take advantage of one's orgasmic potential is, on the one hand, the ability to have multiple orgasms, and, on the other, to master the energy cycle at high levels of arousal. For practice, you can go through the "Whitewater Rapids" kata at the climax of your arousal. In the moment when you flex your PC-muscle, in order to hold back the ejaculation, you pull the energy into the body instead of spilling it out with ejaculation., or centering it in the genitals with the usual multiple orgasm.

At first, you can support this pulling of energy by flexing your large muscle groups. Later, a brief flexing of the PC-muscle and concentration on the top of your skull is usually sufficient for pulling the energy into the head.

Once you've developed this ability, you've reached the highest level of sexual satisfaction. There's very little that could increase your personal ecstasy still further. So now that you're a master of your own body, I'll share a couple more tricks with you in the next chapter as to how you can also satisfy your partner like a true master.

5. Dan - Satisfying Your Partner

Congratulations! You've got all the practical exercises behind you, and are now – if you've completed the program – a master of your own body. You've learned how to observe your arousal, how to control your orgasms, and how to allow your sexual energy to circulate. Perhaps you've also already managed to expand your orgasms to your entire body. I congratulate you on your newfound abilities.

With that, this book has fulfilled its purpose. But since you've been so diligent, you've earned yourself a bonus. Namely, I'll share with you a couple of techniques that will allow you to increase the satisfaction of your partner. As I've said, the practical part is behind you. There are no exercises to go with the following tips. It's left up to you to experiment with them in practice. I wish you – and above all, your partner – a lot of fun doing it.

The Magic Touch

Most men love it when women dive right towards their genitals. Women, on the other hand, often stroke and caress a man generously first, and slowly make their way beneath the belt. This way of proceeding can often drive a strongly aroused man insane. This may not be the optimal way to satisfy a man, but since the woman usually behaves in the way she'd like things done for herself, a careful observation of her actions can tell you a lot about her desires. And so, the first tip: pay attention to how a woman touches you, and give these touches back to her in the same fashion. If you yourself would like to be touched differently, then speak to her about it, and tell her your preferences.

Women often regard it as a bit too direct if you head straight for their genitals, without beating around the bush, so to speak. You should head there only when the woman is sufficiently aroused. You can increase a woman's arousal by touching and caressing the other sensitive points of her body. Her neck, back, the crook of her arm and the hollow of her knee are especially well suited for this. Many women find these touches too ticklish, while for others, it provides an especially pleasant prickling feeling. Here, experimentation is the only thing that will help. The scalp is also very sensible for medium-strength pressure with the fingertips. You can massage it using circular motions, and get the base of the ears involved as well. Most girls also appreciate a bit of passionate hairpulling. Grab a good fist of hair and tenderly pull, so the tension is distributed among a larger surface.

Another important spot is the border between the back and the backside, at the sacral bone. There, where that string-bikini triangle is located, is an area that's accessible to both soft, airy touches and to stronger, massaging stimulation. Once you've done the "Breath of Wind" exercise, then you've surely already gotten to know those spots on your partner's body that really get a reaction out of her.

As soon as your partner is aroused, you can also approach her breasts and genitals. You can notice the increasing excitement in her breathing and in the movement of her body. More on these topics in the following chapters.

Magic Talk

Here's a little trick based on brain research. You surely know that the two halves of the brain are responsible for different tasks. The left hemisphere is used for logical, rational thought, while the right is used for visual, creative thinking.

We'll make use of this circumstance. Many women become aroused if sensual images or exciting words are whispered in their ear. The important thing when doing so is to use language that is as picturesque and emotional as possible, since these sentiments are processed by the right half of the brain.

True, information is processed by both ears, but because of

intersecting (contralateral) processing, the left ear is preferred, since it's in closer contact with the right side of the brain. This has been demonstrated in studies, and one speaks, when referring to the preferred processing of visual information through the left ear, of a "left-ear-advantage" (LEA).

So be sure that you whisper your sweet, dirty talk into your partner's left ear, and select a highly descriptive language!

Most girls are not satisfied with their body features, and are often embarassed to show their body naked for this reason. Help her in asuring her how sexy she looks and how you love to touch her. The tips given in the following chapter apply mostly to all body parts.

The Breasts

The breasts are a touchy issue for many women. The most important rule when dealing with the female breasts involves describing them as perfect if you're asked about them. If she has small breasts, then tell her something like "I prefer cantaloupes to watermelons," or "sure, big today, sagging tomorrow," if the discussion touches on big breasts. If your partner is anywhere above a C-cup, then you'd probably do best to suppress the above-mentioned witticisms. Whatever sort of breasts your partner happens to have, praise them and caress them. Try to emphasize the good parts. If she's got especially pretty nipples, or her bosoms have an especially nice shape when she's standing or lying down, then tell her about it.

When you touch them, do so tenderly at first. Women don't go for sudden groping. Play around the nipples, in ever narrower spirals, with soft, stroking motions. If they get harder, then that's a good indication of their rising arousal. You can then touch the nipples directly, preferably with your tongue, in circular motions.

Unfortunately, one can give no general pieces of advice about the maximum firmness with which one should touch the breasts, since every woman has her particular preferences. Here, it only helps to either ask her about it point-blank, or to increase the intensity until it gets too strong for her. You can share this plan with her ahead of time, and tell her to let you know when things get unpleasant for her, but to give you positive feedback when she especially likes something.

The Genitals

Going about things slowly has also proven itself when it comes to dealing with the genitals. There are, of course, situations of powerful arousal with a trusted partner, when she finds it especially exciting when you grab her right between the legs. But this is a special case, and should by no means become the rule.

First, play around her private parts with strokes on the inside of her upper thigh. While doing so, you can also, as if by accident, touch the labia with the edge of your hand. Then, pass your fingers again from the hipbones up to her mound of Venus. When doing so, vary the pressure and the speed of the motions. Then play a bit with her labia. You can tenderly knead them, rub along them, or gently spread them. By now, she should be very aroused already. When you notice that she's wet enough, you can turn to the clitoris. Otherwise, touching this sensitive spot could be unpleasant or even painful.

The Clitoris

The clitoris is a one-of-a-kind organ, for which there is no male counterpart. The only task of this organ is to feel pleasure. To that end, the clitoris is equipped with a great deal of nerve endings. Rough men's hands have no business there, since most women are extremely sensitive at this spot. If you'd like to pleasure her with your fingers, then you should do so not directly on the clitoris, but slightly above it, so that the pressure won't be too much for her.

For direct stimulation, the tongue is the best-suited tool. Here you can try everything, and observe the reactions of your partner. You can, for example, slightly flap your tongue over the clitoris, or lick over it with the flat surface of your tongue. You can also make circles around the clitoris with the point of your tongue. Alternate between horizontal and vertical movements, and vary the speed. You can also stop briefly (3-5 seconds), only to continue afterwards with faster movements.

Another trick is letter- or number-tonguing. Try to use your tongue to write the numbers from 0 to 10 on the clitoris. That brings some variation to the movements.

Further, you can surround the clitoris with your lips and suck tenderly on it. Be resourceful, and change the direction, pressure, and tempo. Then it shouldn't be much longer before you bring her into ecstasy.

One more important point. Be happy if your woman stimulates her clitoris herself during sex. This causes many men to think that they're not enough for their woman. That's total nonsense. Many women only reach orgasm if the clitoris is given additional stimulation. And if they do it themselves, then she relieves you of the work, because then you don't need to stimulate the clitoris, with optimal pressure, during your thrusts. That's a task that will become harder and harder for you, the closer you get to your own orgasm. Be happy if you've got a partner who's learned to satisfy herself. She can handle this part better than you ever could. After all, she's been practicing for years.

The G-Spot

The G-spot is an erogenous zone of a special kind. Many women find it, but for others it remains an eternal mystery. Named after its discoverer, Ernest Gräfenberg, it's often described as a spot that can bring a women to the utmost ecstasy. Of course, it's not a spot that brings a woman pleasure with the push of a button. The problem that many G-spot searchers have is that they may know more or less where it's located, but they have no idea how to handle it.

But first let's clear up where it is exactly. The place is located 4-5 cm inside the vagina, on the upper side, behind the pubic bone. To search for it, you can insert the index or middle finger into the vagina, with your palm facing upwards. Look for a slightly furrowed or coarse place that lies on a sort of cord.

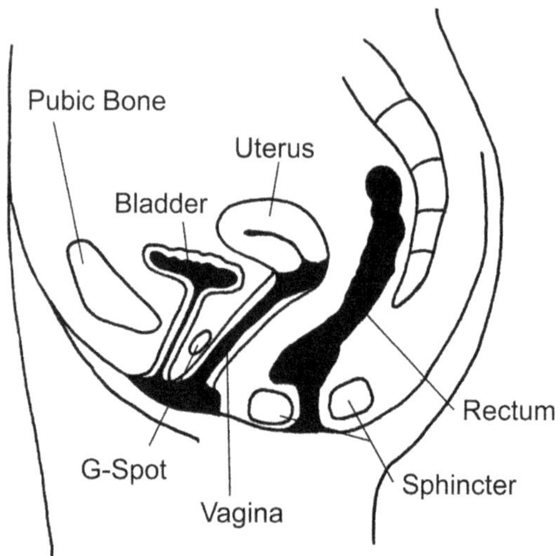

Illustration 12: Location of the G-spot

Now that the "where" has been cleared up, it's time to get to the bottom of the "how" and the "when." Because that's the real secret that causes so many seekers to fail. Namely, the G-spot only reveals itself as an erogenous zone if the woman is already powerfully aroused. Then, it becomes a sort of afterburner that can only be ignited at high speeds.

It can be located best directly following an orgasm, since at that time, this area is highly engorged with blood. If you were to apply the arousal scale to your woman, then you shouldn't stimulate the G-spot before level 8. Before, it may be that it's unpleasant for your partner, or that she doesn't feel anything at all. Much as a light stroking near the clitoris is already too much for many women, while others need a strong pressure before they feel anything at all. Here, the only thing that will help is experimenting and communicating. One thing that's proven its value is a light tapping at one-second intervals. But here, too, variation wins the day. So try out different rhythms, with varying pressure, and don't be disappointed if your partner's reactions are different than those promised by many myths.

Penetration

Once you've pleasured the woman with your fingers and mouth, the best part comes into play. But before you plunge right in with your bottlenosed dolphin, you should frolic around with it a bit on the surface. For example, rub your penis on top of the clitoris. Either horizontally, or with circular movements, you can arouse your partner to such a degree that she can barely wait for you to penetrate her.

When things have come this far, then proceed slowly, bit by bit. Two steps forward, one step back. In that way, you'll stimulate your partner further, and her desire will only increase. Once you've left her hanging for a bit in this fashion, pull your penis back once more, before plunging into her, slowly, but ever deeper. Be sure not to hurt her, especially if you've got a whopping big member.

What you can then do with your penis, once you've started diving, you'll learn in the following chapter.

Thrust Techniques

"Wham, bam, thank you ma'am!" Now that you've got your black belt in the MO-technique, this phrase should be a thing of the past for you.

As always, a little variety goes a long way here. So you should, in any case, alter your rhythm. In the arousal phase, you'll have considerably more success if the woman isn't able to get used to the rhythm. But if your partner is headed towards orgasm, it may help her if you maintain your rhythm over longer phases, so that she can get involved with it.

With deep thrusts, the shaft of your penis will be stimulated over the entire length of its path. This has a positive effect for erectile difficulties, but can make it difficult to control your orgasm. The Taoists suggest alternating between 9 shallow and one deep thrust. I suggest that you find your own rhythm. Find which thrust techniques are especially exciting for you, and which feel comfortable over longer phases.

The vagina expands inside the woman's body like a hollow. Moreover, the length of its walls are all equipped with erogenous zones of varying intensity. So try to reach different corners with your penis (both vertically and horizontally), in order to reach as many points as possible (shotgun system). Observe the reactions of your partner in order to find out which spots are especially arousing for her. Then you can zero in and sniper them.

When you've got a strong erection, then you can also grab the penis at its base and move it in circling, stirring motions.

A further technique is screwing. Here, the penis isn't simply pushed in and out, but, during penetration, is "screwed" in with circular movements of the pelvis. If you keep your hips moving, you can really pleasure your partner. During screwing, alternate the direction of the movement, in order to provide for even more variation.

Positions

If you're interested in varied or acrobatic positions, then I suggest the Kama Sutra or other erotic books that have specialized in this topic. Here, I'd only like to go into a couple of basic positions, and their advantages and disadvantages.

In Taoism, concerning this matter, there are several interesting theories. Touching with the same body parts (for example, hands, lips or genitals) provide relaxation and for the restoration of harmony. Real arousal comes when different body parts touch each other (for example, lips and ear, lips and genitals, etc.). Beyond that, the active partner donates energy to the passive partner.

Let's now look at three basic positions, with regard to arousal and orgasm control.

Man on Top

If the man's on top, then we're usually dealing with some variation of the classic missionary position. An important advantage of this position lies in the fact that the partners are facing each other. This enables eye contact and kissing. In addition, your partner can embrace you and stroke you along your spine, in order to promote the flow of energy.

In order to reach the G-spot with your penis in this position, the woman must place a pillow beneath her pelvis. That way, the man can push into her at a steeper angle. The higher she lifts her legs, the deeper the penetration will be. Therefore this technique is especially recommended if the woman has a rather large vagina, or the man has a somewhat smaller penis. This position becomes difficult for the man if he supports himself with his arms. It's significantly less demanding to kneel in front of the woman, upright and with your legs spread. That way, the man can control both the angle and the depth of the penetration in optimal fashion. Further his hands are free for additional manual stimulation.

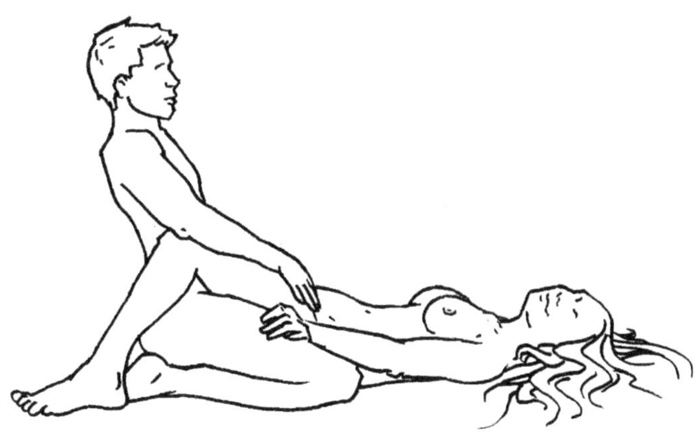

Illustration 13: Position - Man on Top

Woman on Top

This position is especially nice for orgasm control, since you can relax completely and concentrate on your arousal curve. Most men are especially successful in become multiorgasmic in this position.

A further advantage lies in the fact that the woman has control over the angle and depth of the penetration. That way, she can direct the penis towards the sensitive areas inside her vagina. This position is therefore the most orgasm-friendly for most women.

On top of that, the man has his hands free, and can stroke or stimulate his partner. One trick in this position is to lay one hand flat on the stomach right above the penis. Your fingers should point in the direction of the penis, and the middle finger should touch its base. If your hand is in the right place, then your partner can rub with her clitoris directly over the knuckle of the back side of your finger. While doing so, she can determine the pressure and movement herself, and you can additionally carry out wave-like movements with your hand to offer her support.

Illustration 14: Position - Woman on Top

Man from Behind

This position is also known in common parlance as “doggy-style.” Here, the woman kneels in front of her partner and sticks her rear end towards him. The man penetrates her from behind. Here, the woman’s vagina is especially narrow, which makes orgasm-control more difficult. This position is therefore especially good for the initial phase of lovemaking, when the arousal is still less. Also, in the case of a small penis and a big vagina, this position can be recommended, since the friction is increased due to the narrowness.

True, the partners can’t look at each other, or kiss, but the man has his hands free to stroke his partner, or to massage her breasts.

If you’d like to ride the rodeo, you can also grab her hair in this position, penetrate her deeply, and then tell her that sex with her is almost as good as with that new intern at the office. Let’s just see how long you can hold on after that.

Illustration 15: Position - Man from behind

6. Dan – Sexualization of the Spirit

The Yin and Yang is the ancient Asian symbol for two parts that together make a whole. The Yin stands for the female energy of the universe, and the Yang for the male counterpart. But there are still more meanings ascribed to the two sides – for example, hot and cold, or light and dark.

Illustration 16: Yin and Yang

In every person, both energies are found – male and female. At the highest levels of sexual arousal, an energy exchange takes place between the two partners. During it, the energy circulates through the two partners, and becomes stronger. Such an energy exchange, however, can't be experienced during a one-night stand, since an exchange like this requires a great level of intimacy. Besides, both partners must master the energy flow through their own body, before they can make the transition to exchanging energy.

First, try to harmonize your breathing. Embrace each other so that your heads are lying beside each other. That way, you can mutually hear your breath, and try to align it.

You can imagine giving forth hot male Yang-energy through your penis, which your partner then absorbs. In exchange, you can pull the cool, female Yin energy from her vagina and send it up your spine, in the energy cycle. If the two of you have built up and exchanged sufficient energy through prolonged lovemaking, then it will reach your head, where you can allow it to circulate. Now, the energy can be either diverted as usual into the stomach area, or be exchanged at the head level through kisses and the touching of the tongues.

Each partner should then divert the energy arriving through the tongue down to the navel, in order to store it there.

It will take a little time until the two of you learn to handle the various energies. But if you succeed, you'll be rewarded with an experience that will provide you with tremendous intimacy and a genuinely electrifying feeling of pleasure.

7. Sexual Problems

Most men have sexual problems at some point in their lives. Maybe you've also had erectile difficulties at a decisive moment, or worry about your penis size. Many men suffer from premature ejaculation, and others have prostate problems.

This chapter is dedicated to the most common problems you'll encounter during sex.

Premature Ejaculation

The exercise program of this book is aimed at better controlling your arousal and orgasms. If you've done the exercises and have thereby gained control over your body, then this problem may well be a thing of the past.

If you've reached the master level, then you've also experienced the Taoist path. This calls for completely avoiding ejaculation, and ejaculating only once a month in order to relieve surplus energy. According to this view, most men have premature ejaculation by definition. Ejaculation is no longer the goal – only the orgasm is. Once you've learned the MO-technique, then, in the future, it's left up to you if you'd like to experience ejaculation.

It can, of course, always happen that, in the heat of battle, you fire too quickly. Don't worry about it. We're only men, not machines. You've learned techniques in the previous chapter, with which you can send a woman into ecstasy even without your penis.

Impotence

Most men have erectile difficulties at some point in their lives. That's completely normal, and I'd even be worried if that weren't the case. It's important to understand that erectile difficulties have nothing to do with impotence. Erectile difficulties can have any number of causes, since an erection is a complex interplay of various processes. Stress, performance pressure, tiredness, alcohol or over-exertion are only a few of the reasons why your colleague won't rise to the task.

Prolonged impotence usually has biological reasons. If you're no longer sure whether you're capable of getting an erection, then you can conduct a simple test. Since men, more often than not, get an erection during sleep, you can, before going to bed, stick a row of postal stamps to your penis. If it's torn the next morning, then that's a sign that you are at least biologically capable of getting an erection.

The most common reason for erectile difficulty is a lack of self-confidence. If you're already afraid of not getting an erection, then this often becomes a self-fulfilling prophecy, and a vicious circle. But learning the MO-technique should have brought you some clarity regarding your sexual abilities. So don't worry too much about your penis, but more about your woman. Use the techniques from the previous chapter. Rest content in the assurance that you can satisfy a woman even without sexual intercourse. That will take the pressure off your penis. It will soon feel left out, and will be dying to join in the fun.

A further technique you can apply is soft penetration. According to the motto: soft in, hard out. For that, you partner must be very wet, so stimulate her sufficiently beforehand, or use a lubricating fluid. The technique works best if you lie on top, since gravity will help you to gather blood in your penis. Close your thumb and index finger into a ring that you then place around your penis, squeezing slightly. That way, blood and energy will be drawn into the penis and held there. Then, guide your penis carefully into your partner, and begin with some gentle thrusts. Continue to hold the ring closed. Visualize how blood and energy are streaming into your penis. You can support this with contractions of the butt-cheeks and of the PC-muscle. Adjust the pressure of your ring in such a way that the swelling is enough for the thrusting, and let up on the ring as soon as your penis is hard enough.

The certainty of being able to perform this technique should give you additional self-confidence, and thus, nip the psychological problem in the bud.

Sperm Count

One often reads or hears of a troubling decrease in sperm count in many men. Above all in industrialized countries, the average sperm count has fallen by up to 50%. The reasons for this are numerous, and range from pants that are too tight to chemical pollution. Problems arise for couples concerned with having children. A low sperm count is, however, no conclusive sign of infertility, even if doctors may frequently make this diagnosis.

With the master levels of the MO-technique, you've learned techniques for restraining your ejaculations. If you'd like to raise your sperm count, then you should in any case use this technique. Every day without an ejaculation increases your sperm count by 50-90 million. It would be nice if the balance of your bank account would rise in this way, but not even a sperm bank will help you there.

You should additionally make the switch to boxer shorts in order to give Mr. Public Prosecutor a little room to operate, and provide him with an energizing massage every now and then.

The Prostate

Prostate cancer is one of the most common maladies for men. In the US, almost every tenth man receives this diagnosis over the course of his life. Most men only begin thinking about their prostate when trouble arises.

Through the MO-technique, you've taken an important step for the health of your prostate. PC-training massages the prostate, and helps with its blood circulation. If you get the prostate involved as an erogenous zone, then the positive effect rises even higher.

So, even after the strengthening of your PC-muscle, you should continue the exercises as a maintenance measure. For this, the exercises "Stop the Stream" and the "PC-jabs" work especially well.

If you have problems with your prostate, then you should apply the finger-stop from the chapter "Point of a million gold coins" during the brown belt.

Penis Size

"Size does matter," we're constantly told. Therefore, men with a small penis frequently have problems and are ashamed in the dressing room and in the bedroom. But men with a penis that is too large often have problems as well, since it's often simply too much of a good thing for many women.

I'd advise against an operation, since these lead to complications more often than you'd think. And what man wants complications in this realm? But I'll give you an exercise you can use to enlarge your penis by up to 2.5 centimeters.

Ever received a penis-enlargement-spam-email? Forget all mails that offer you pills or other treatments for a lot of money, in order to increase the size of your penis. Here, you'll find methods that many dealers sell in different variations, for big bucks – but in this book it's a free bonus and my personal payback to penis-enlargement-spam.

But before I get to this exercise, I've got a few more bits of advice for you, if your penis is too big or too small.

In the "Positions" chapter, I've already given you a few tips as to which positions are optimal for a smaller penis. But the arousal of your partner is also of decisive importance for her subjective feeling. When aroused, the vagina becomes more engorged with blood, which causes it to swell. Therefore, the penis is felt by the woman to be bigger. So make sure that your partner is sufficiently aroused before you enter her. The majority of sensations take place in the front part of the vagina. Therefore, if you apply it correctly, you can satisfy a woman with a small penis too. Always keep in mind that a small penis, with the right technique, satisfies a woman more than a big but inexperienced penis. „All the gear but no idea" is simply unsatisfying.

Many women get scared if the penis is too big. If you're well-endowed, you can relieve your partner's fears, and give yourself more control, by tying a band (for example, a shoelace) around your erect member. That way, you can establish the maximum depth to which you can penetrate your woman. For big fellahs, I recommend the "woman on top" position as the optimal one. That way, she has the control over the depth and angle of the penetration. Your job is, even in the heat of battle, not to thrust too powerfully.

Penis Enlargement

First of all, you should know that the entire MO-technique training has a positive effect on penis size. Since for many men who are less sexually active the penis becomes pulled back into the body, the portion of it that is visible shrinks. By strengthening your PC-muscles and the other pelvic muscles, your penis is pressed further out of your body, and the result is an optical penis enlargement.

With the following exercise, you can take the enlargement of your penis even further. Depending on the starting condition, you can add as much as 2.5 centimeters. In order to control for penis size, you can measure your penis beforehand, and then follow your growth over time. Always measure yourself in the same way – best of all, on the upper side, from the base to the tip. You can use a measuring tape, a ruler, or a piece of cord. Don't forget to measure the girth.

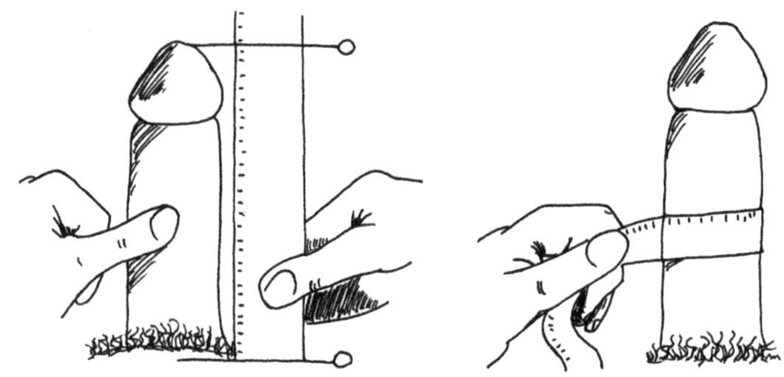

Illustration 17: Measure your Penis

This is the only technique that I can't confirm through personal experience – enough is enough. But many men report success with the following technique, so, in any case, it's worth a try, if you're pursuing this goal.

It's of no use if you only apply the technique off and on. If you really want to enlarge your penis, then you should let the following exercises become a habit, and integrate them into your daily routine – for example, after showering. Do the exercises at least 5 times per week. Then you'll notice after 2-4 weeks that your penis is becoming thicker and longer. After 3-4 weeks, you'll detect a clear enlargement, and the enlargement will be permanent.

If you feel pains during these exercises, then let it proceed a bit more loosely. There's no reason for pain, since penis enlargement doesn't hurt.

In order to get the most out of the exercises, you should get the proper nourishment. Make sure to take in all of the important building blocks of nutrition (protein, carbohydrates, vitamins, minerals, etc.). It would be a shame if you limited your growth by some lack of nutrition. Besides that, you should drink plenty of water.

View it as a real workout. If you're reading this program for fun, you might think that the training is too time-intensive. But if you seriously have the goal to get a larger penis, then it should be well worth the effort.

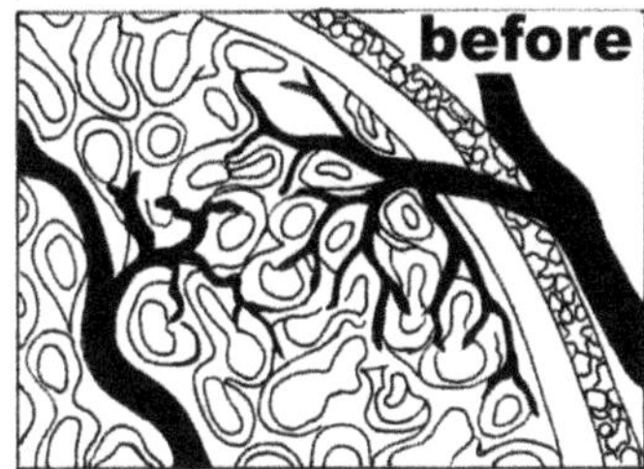

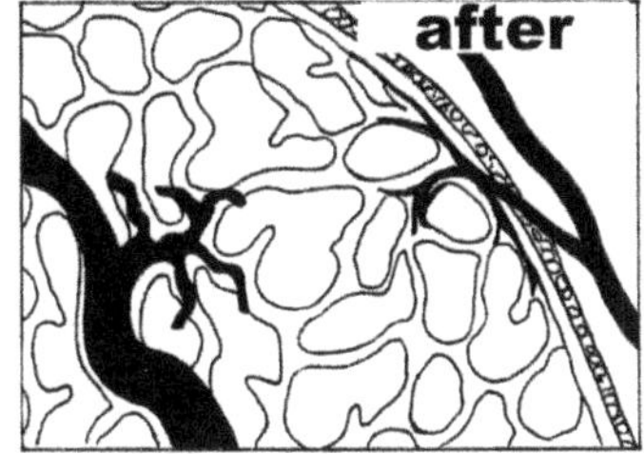

Illustration 18:
Corpus cavernosum cells before and after the workout

You should begin each session with a hot dog:

Hot Dog

I've given the name "hot dog" to the hot wrap that should be applied before every exercise. It's not half as dramatic as it sounds. Take a washcloth and soak it with hot water for a few seconds. Wring out the excess water, and lay the washcloth around your penis. Allow the warmth to soak in for 2-3 minutes. Repeat the steps until your penis is nicely warm and relaxed. Then dry it off well, so that you can grab it tightly during the following exercises.

Tug-Of-War

This exercise serves to lengthen the penis. The tissue is made to expand, which creates lengthening in both flaccid and erect states. The penis won't become thicker through this exercise. You carry out this exercise while seated on the edge of something, or while standing.

1. The penis should be flaccid and well warmed ahead of time when you begin the exercise. Grab it with a firm grip in the area of the shaft, but not so firmly as to make it uncomfortable. Support the grip with your second hand, in order to keep a confident hold on things.
2. Pull the penis lengthwise away from your body. Regulate the strength so that you can notice a stretching of the penis without pain. Hold the stretch for 30 seconds and repeat it ten times, each time a bit stronger.
3. Relax and flap your penis around a bit. Give yourself some applause by clapping it against your legs. This increases the blood circulation. Afterwards, relax for a minute.
4. Repeat the steps above, each time with a different tugging direction: to the left, to the right, upwards and downwards.
5. Close out the exercise by moving the penis around in a circle while pulling. 30 times clockwise, then 30 times counter-clockwise.
6. Relax the penis with step three, and a quick hot dog.

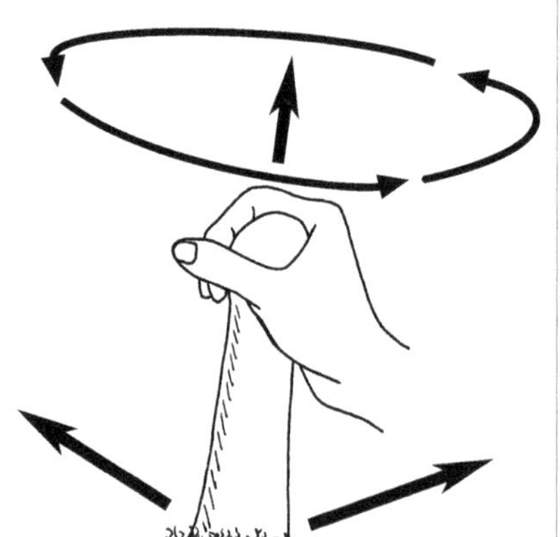

Illustration 19: Tug-Of-War

Penis Milking

The milking of the penis has already been practiced for hundreds of years by many cultures and tribes. As a family secret this knowledge was often passed from father to son. Milking is counted as the most effective technique for the permanent enlargement of the penis – both in terms of length and of girth.

Through milking, blood is pressed into the vessels of the part of the penis that swells. After a few months of daily practice, these vessels are expanded, which leads to an increased absorption capacity. This leads to a permanent enlargement.

For this exercise, you absolutely need a lubricant. You should either sit or stand, so that the penis can be milked downwards. By not lying down, the exercise is supported by gravity.

You should have three-fourths erection in order to milk. It's not too productive to milk a flaccid penis, since there's hardly any blood in it. So first stimulate yourself until you have a level 5-7 erection.

Then, close the ring formed from your thumb and index finger, as if you're making the OK-sign. Draw up the ring with medium to strong pressure and move it in the direction of the tip of the penis.

In so doing, press the blood in the shaft into the head of the penis. You can observe, when moving the ring downwards, an enlargement of the head of the penis. Alternate your hands, so that you can perform a continuous milking motion.

In the beginning, you should milk 100-200 times; that is, for approximately 10 minutes. After a couple of days, you can increase to 20 or even a maximum of 30 minutes. After 2 weeks at the most, you should be able to measure a significant difference. After 3-4 months, your success will become permanent.

I wish you a lot of fun with your penis upgrade.

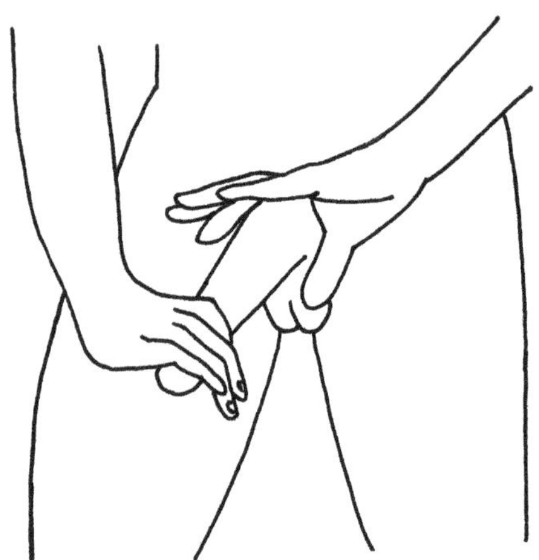

Illustration 20: Penis Milking

8. Afterword

I hope you've had fun with this book and the practices it contains. If you've completed the program, then it won't be long until you master the MO-technique. It's left up to you whether or not you have the ambition to push forward into the master level. But even if you've "only" managed the black belt, your sexual experiences will reach a substantially higher level. In this, you belong to that rare tribe of MO-men who have overcome those struggles required to become a better lover and give their partner better sex. Every woman who profits from this should count herself lucky, especially if you've learned the technique for her sake.

I hope you liked the way in which I've revealed the secrets of the multiple orgasm to you. I thank you for having purchased this book, and hope that I've fulfilled your expectations. I'm sure that the value this book can have for you will justify the investment, in any case.

On my web site, www.mancan.net, I offer my readers a forum where they can share their experiences, tips and tricks, exercise variations, and, of course, criticism. Access to the forum is restricted to the readers of this book, and is therefore password-protected.

The password is: MOForum (case sensitive!)

You can also send me your experiences, suggestions, and critiques by e-mail, at feedback@mancan.net

Lots of success during your training, and don't forget:

Flex the PC-muscle!

Bibliography

[1] Robbins, M.B. and Jensen, G.D.: Multiple Orgasms in Males, in: Journal of Sex Research 14 (1978), pp 21-26
(on of the first scientific articles on the male multiple orgasm).

[2] Hartman, W. and Fithian, M.: Any Man Can, New York 1984.
(One of the first books on the topic, with tips on possible learning methods. Many anecdotes from sexual therapy).

[3] Ladas, A., Kahn, A., Whipple, B. and Perry, J.: The G-Spot and Other Recent Discoveries About Human Sexuality, New York 1993.
(Publications on the female G-spot).

[4] Keesling, B.: How to Make Love All Night…, 1995.
(This is the book that led me to the multiple orgasm. Unfortunately, no longer available in German).

[5] Chia, M. and Arava, D. A.: The Multi-Orgasmic Man (Sexual Secrets Every Man Should Know), 1997 .
(A very good book on sexual Tao Multiple orgasms through the control of sexual energy. Recommended for deepening the master level).

Further Reading:

Anand, M.: The Art of Sexual Ecstasy, 1989.
(For black belts. Practices for handling sexual energy)

Brauer, A., Brauer, D.: ESO Extended Sexual Orgasm, 1989. (Interesting reading with lots of orgasm exercises for men and women).

Chang, J.: The Tao of Love and Sex, the Ancient Chinese Way to Ecstasy, New York 1977. (The standard work on the sexual aspect of Taoism).

Douglas, N. and Shigis, P.: Sexual Secrets: The Alchemy of Ecstasy, New York 1979.

Dunn, M. and Trost, J.: Male Multiple Orgasms: A Descriptive Study, in: Archives of Sexual Behavior 18(5), pp 377-387.
(Scientific work on the male multiple orgasm)

Masters, W., Johnson, V. and Kolodny, R.: Love and Sexuality, Berlin 1993. (the standard work on the topic of love and sexuality)

Paget, L.: The Perfect Lover, Munich 2001. (Many tips for men, unfortunately with no mention of the multiple orgasm).